Birth of a Tribe

Memoir
Paraka Nii

PAUL PURI NII

Papua New Guinea

Copyright © Paul Puri Nii 2023

All rights reserved. No part of this book may be reproduced or transmitted in any form or by any means, electronic or mechanical, including photocopying, recording or by any information storage and retrieval system, without prior written permission of the Publisher below. The Australian Copyright Act 1968 allows one chapter only, or 10% of this book, whichever is the greater, to be photocopied by any educational institution for its educational purposes provided that the educational institution (or body that administers it) has given a copyright notice to the Copyright Agency (Australia) under the Act.

Paperback ISBN: 978-0-6459322-2-5

First Published in 2023 by

First Nations Writers Festival International Limited

T/as First Nations Publishers

A Registered Charity (ABN 79 655 932 979)

2/53 Junction St, Nowra NSW 2540, Australia

Phone: +61 491 851 353

Email: firstnationswritersfestival@gmail.com

Web: www.firstnationswritersfestival.org

FB: www.facebook.com/firstnationswritersfestival.com

Cover Design: Tim Axton

Typesetting: Busybird Publishing

Line Edited: Anna Borzi AM 2023

Printed and bound in Australia by IngramSpark

This book is a MEMOIR

As told to, as heard by, and as witnessed by

the extensive family of, and fellow tribe members of

Chief of the Grand Companion of the Order of Logohu

as appointed on 43rd Independence Anniversary

of Papua New Guinea

as appointed by

Her Majesty, Elizabeth II Queen of Papua New Guinea.

Chief Paraka Nii
(1939 – 2021)

My uncle was my grandmother's first son. My grandmother was a devoted Christian of the Baptist faith, after the Australian Baptist Missionaries came to Baiyer river. Prior to this she believed entirely in her custom instincts. My grandmother was an exceptional illustration of a God-fearing woman whose cultural norms cannot command her faith for God.

My father and my uncle were her favourite sons, she would spend a lot of time teaching them of the word of God, and how they would manage their lives guided by the word of God. As a child, I too became absorbed in my grandmother's love for God. Paraka Nii was too. On the other hand, he was looked upon by all the children of his other brothers as a father and mentor who stood by his stringent disciplines to shape the current tribe of Kyakin in the Sip lineage to the one of the role model tribes in the whole of the Western Highlands and Papua New Guinea.

Apart from my father, I received most of the disciplines and encouragement in life from my uncle and my grandmother, and therefore my current life is a reflection of their inputs. My uncle and grandmother kept on telling me that road to success in life comes from those who believe in God, and honour their parents, and remain humble themselves, and study hard. I have wholeheartedly embraced their advice and my existing life is an unswerving testament of their philosophy. Thus, I am indebted to not being thankful enough.

This is their story.

Contents

FOREWORD 1

CHAPTER 1
GREAT WARRIOR NII 3

CHAPTER 2
HIS BRIDE LENGAME 13

CHAPTER 3
ANCESTORS 15

CHAPTER 4
PARAKA'S BIRTH 21

CHAPTER 5
CHILDHOOD ON THE MOUNTAINS 31

CHAPTER 6
ARRIVAL OF THE WHITE MEN 37

CHAPTER 7
ENROLLED AT MISSION SCHOOL 45

CHAPTER 8
WORKED WITH THE AUSTRALIAN FARMERS 51

CHAPTER 9
PARENTS DIVORCED 61

CHAPTER 10
PIGS, LAND & WIVES 71

CHAPTER 11
WHITE MEN INTRODUCE LOCAL GOVERNMENT 81

CHAPTER 12
WESTERN HIGHLANDS PROVINCIAL POLITICS 93

CHAPTER 13
WESTERN HIGHLANDS POLITICS 103

CHAPTER 14
PUBLIC SERVICE 111

CHAPTER 15
COUNCIL PRESIDENT 117

VOCABULARY 123

WITH THANKS 127

PHOTOS 131

FOREWORD

First Nations Writers Festival – the Greater Pacific awarded Mr Nii a FNWF2023 Book award for this memoir. The Judges said "Most if not all history of Papua New Guinea is written by or about the Kiaps or the Missionaries. Colonialists. Not about the experiences or history of the citizens away from the white gaze."

"Fortunately, just as knowledge of the first encounters are held in the precarious hands of Elders, these experiences are being written. They are important. They are precious. This memoir of a mother and her son, is a re-writing of history, using the words of the protagonist, the family, the village, the entire Highlands – and Country. As it should be. A mighty effort to cover over 100 years in the living right up to an award of Grand Companion of the Order of Logohu, as Chief, in 2018 to the son, the highest award in PNG. A mighty life recorded here and shared. A mighty family, village and country. Compelling history. As it would be. This book amplifies the voices of the peoples of PNG."

Paul Puri Nii comes from Kuipboat village in the Kyakin tribe of Baiyer District in Western Highlands Province, PNG. He has a Bachelor of Laws degree from the University of Papua New Guinea and a Master of Laws Degree with Honors from the University of Waikato in NZ. He is currently the Principal Magistrate of the District Courts of PNG. This is his first novel.

Thank you to Mr Nii, his family and community for this important history.

In this Memoir, Mr Nii shares his Grandmother's, and his Uncles' stories, and in so doing, shares his own and the history of PNG.

Shape shifting from fantasy and myths of creation of this new tribe; the intellectual strengths that underpinned the cultural resilience to sustain it; and the assimilation (mostly) with the first colonisers when they arrived. The full arc of life is explored from a remote part of PNG to the centre of the new capital of the new country with a new Queen.

It is important to appreciate the scale of this memoir. His uncle, Paraka is the first-born son of this new tribe, in a remote village in the Highlands. Born twelve years after the birth of HRH Princess Elizabeth in 1927; who would survive her own tribal power-struggles in the UK at that time, and eventually become Her Majesty the Queen of Papua New Guinea.

Nothing could have foreshadowed this relationship for Her Majesty nor for Paraka, living in this remote village. But their lives were closely entwined. By the time both passed in the early 2020's, PNG had become independent and a member of the Commonwealth, and Mr Paraka Nii, had been awarded by Her Majesty the Queen, an MBE 1995 (Member British Empire); Silver Jubilee Medal 2000; and 30-year Independence Anniversary Medal 2005 for his contribution to the people of PNG.

And Paraka Nii was elevated to the highest Honour of all by his Queen for his country: Papua New Guinea. This is the story of the mother, her wish and its fulfilment. AB

CHAPTER 1

GREAT WARRIOR NII

"The bride price is kina shells, dorm pigs, bird of paradise plumes and bamboo containers of crude oil".

The famous warrior Nii lowered his head in consideration at this demand. His desired bride was worth the price he decided.

He had lifted his stone axe, landed it heavily on Pombra Kit, the leader of the enemy tribe, and chopped his head off with blood spraying over the ground at his feet.

As a result of his actions a full-scale tribal war flared through the Western Highlands of Papua New Guinea, not for the first time, nor the last. But it was from the recent fighting that he had earned his reputation as a skilful, fearless warrior, attracting numerous women hungry for his name and protection.

It was Lengame who crowded his thoughts after meeting her at a Tanim Het for Lengame's girlfriend, Rongo. More than one man had composed a song for the courtship ceremony to convince Rongo to choose him for her husband.

Rongo, an albino, had run away from her husband and her life in the thick jungles of the West not far from where the fat, long-eared people lived. When she returned to her people's village, they sat wide-eyed listening to her tale.

"Life was busy and interesting as weeks and months passed until it occurred to me that my husband often went missing in the night as I slept. Each night I fell into despair when I stretched out my arms and legs in the hope of enjoying each other's love, only to find him missing. Fear and suspicion invaded my thoughts making me physically ill at times. Why would a lovely handsome man abandon me on the bed, I continually asked myself."

As she sipped her cold drink, Rongo continued with her tale.

"One day my husband and I went into the midst of the jungle to plant a garden. We had banana suckers, sugar cane stalks and other necessary seedlings in our bilums. After a morning of heavy work we were both very tired and hungry so we stopped to cook food for lunch under the shade of a large tree.

While I was preparing the food, my husband climbed a nearby tree to gather more mushrooms. Noticing the silence I raised my head to check on my husband who I could not see. What I could see was a huge, long snake. I shouted and cried out in fear. The snake abruptly uncoiled itself and glided down the tree towards me making scary hissing sounds while poking its dirty ugly tongue out with every hiss. Shivering in fear in front of the snake, I heard the snake speak. "I am your husband".

I watched in awe as the snake changed its physical appearance with my husband's face appearing on the head of the snake. The rest of my husband's body appeared gradually. The afternoon gardening activities were disturbed by this frightful experience so we headed home looking in different directions without even saying a word to each other.

I was so worried that I had married a man who could sometimes easily change to the form of an animal that I decided I would leave my husband during the night while he was absent. After a dinner of highland sweet potatoes and some pitpit we went to bed to sleep. When I woke I was not surprised to find that my husband was gone again. I quietly crept out of our house surrounded by thick forest and began to run fast following a small track in the jungle. In the black of night I stumbled frequently, hitting my feet against the roots of the trees. My body would react to the eerie noises made by the forest animals but the fear of my husband overcame these fears.

Rongo's relatives hugged and kissed her as her tears rolled down her cheeks. After their strong insistence that she not return to her husband, Rongo listened to them and stayed in her village adjacent to the stone bridge of the Baiyer River. It wasn't long before Rongo would go out in the night to meet men from the neighbouring tribes. There was no restriction on the number of men who could court these ladies so both attracted many suitors. Her cousin Lengame joined her and it was Lengame that warrior Nii wanted for his bride.

He began his courtship of Lengame as music filled the night air and bodies danced to the primal beat of the drums. Before the Tanim Het proceeded, a huge bond fire was lit inside the house and people sat around it singing songs. After the house was warm enough, the fire was put out and small dried pitpit sticks were lit to provide a dim light just enough to see each other's faces, similar to disco lights provided on a dance floor. Couples at the Tanim Het sat with their legs crisscrossed facing each other. Heads turn to the right, heads turn to the left, back to face the front, both nodding forward to touch each other's nose. Around them the spectators sang songs of love while emotions and connections flare between the courting couples. Some would recognise their future life partner; some would know they were with the wrong person and try again and possibly again at future Tanim Het courtship occasions.

Lengame's initial hesitancy to Nii's approaches was drowned by the continual encouragement of her brothers, Gaiyer and Lipu.

"He will protect you. Marry him".

Stories of his tribal fighting and hunting were told around the fires at night through many villages. From his teenage years through manhood Nii would go secretly to distant villages, kill a man and bring back his armband, beads off his hat as proof of his strength and bravery.

Lengame listened, but also thought of her first husband.

Laniyoko, Chief of the Maranyi tribe and mortal enemies of the Ukuni tribe, sat with his other two wives in their house built of kunai grasses, planning the next day's activities. It was a warm and cloudless night unlike the other nights of the month. The insects had finished their chirping while an eastern breeze blew softly from the Baiyer gorge across the valley.

Smoke haze drifted from the west from where it was rumoured that the long and wide eared people of the Ukuni tribe lived. It was said that they used their ears as blankets and mats to cover their bodies when they went to sleep. Mothers would chant tales of such people to their children who refused to go to bed.

This night Laniyoko sensed danger signalled by the varying noises of night creatures. He told Lengame and his other two wives "it is likely that the enemies are going to come here tonight," he said bravely. "You ladies should go and hide somewhere."

His wives reluctantly accepted his precautionary command.

"If we are go, where you are intending to stay?" the concerned wives asked.

"I am a man. I will stay here tonight to fight back," Laniyoko answered courageously. "If I get killed I'll die, but you must go somewhere, where you all will be safe."

Two of his wives refused to do as they were told and stayed with Laniyoko in their haus man clinging to his legs saying they would rather die with him.

Lengame listened once and then moved. She walked quietly down an uneven hill and at last made her way into the pigs' sty making sure not to disturb the sleeping pigs. She found an empty room and laid down on the cold dry grasses where the pigs slept. Only the incessant insects broke the quiet. She could hardly bear the terrible smell of the pig's urine and faeces and found it extremely difficult to sleep in this unbearable situation. The words of her husband repeatedly filled her mind but sleep finally came.

As Lengame slept, something strange happened. She felt something cold sitting on her bare chest and woke up suddenly to hear some men talking outside the pigpen. Very cautiously she lifted her head to hear what the men were saying.

"Ela omba ken kand ken mul,". Melpa language meaning that whoever was inside will escape so watch carefully.

When Lengame heard that statement she knew right away that they were the enemy. With terrified feelings, she almost fainted but slowly recouped her conscious thought, courageously jumping to her feet and walked quietly towards the door. Peeping through the small holes she could easily figure out the shadows of men standing in a straight line. Armed with spears above their shoulders they were prepared to shoot at anything that moved out of the sty. Lengame knew very well that if she remained, the Melpa language-speaking warriors would shoot her. She was a woman. The customary belief in most Highlands society was that a woman might give birth to a boy who could later retaliate as a warrior. So women were easily killed without a second thought.

Faced with the critical decision as to whether to escape or remain in the sty and get killed Lengame finally decided that she should try escape by running out of the sty. Very quietly she moved aside the pieces of wood that were used to keep the pigs contained. Moving stealthily out of the entrance she ran as fast as her legs could carry her, faster than a young man. Some of the enemy tribe threw spears aiming to kill her but fortunately missed her. She ran all the way down to a small creek, crossed the creek, and climbed a plateau, as screams of women and children reached her. Turning to view the scene Lengame saw houses in flames. She hoped that it was not her beloved husband and the wives that may have been killed in the attack. Despondently she continued walking until she came to the village of one of her distant cousins who accommodated her for the night. Sleep evaded her after what she had been through that night, of the screams she had heard and the houses she saw in flames.

Very early the next morning the songs of the birds woke Lengame who went outside to see what was happening. A huge grey cloud hovered in the direction of the sun and blocked its rays. It was the first time she had witnessed such a thing. Horrified at the scene, she stood still with tears falling. The clouds and smoke haze moved away making way for the sun's rays. The terrible news she was anticipating reached her. Laniyoko and his two wives who stayed with him had been killed during the night. Lengame wept bitterly as she gazed towards the destroyed village. Later that day, her brothers Gaiyer and Lipu arrived to rescue her and travelled together back to their village. Lengame soon settled into village life taking on the chores of a woman.

The question she asked herself each evening as she settled was should she accept the warrior Nii Laik from the Kyakini tribe as her husband. Tribal fights were a way of life, a way of settling disputes to earn peace and stories of Nii Laik's bravery abounded.

Another brave warrior from Nii's tribe, Kyawaleta, had sneaked into enemy territory one night. He crept cautiously towards the akala anda, the men's house where the enemy was staying. pretending to be one of their tribesmen and called out in a deep voice.

'Wane o, namba yanda pimuai akali eparami lao iso karo kande, nakamba paliyapa,'

("I'm on guard tonight so rest in peace,")

One of the men in the akali anda, thought that the person talking outside was his tribesman or from an allied tribe. He walked out to greet him. Kyawaleta instantly killed the man with a spear, piercing the enemy's heart who died instantly so had not yelled out any warning. A second man standing outside suffered a similar fate with a spear penetrating his body. He then set the akali anda on fire and stood at the doorway killing each man as he rushed from the burning house. None of them were able to attack him because they were all tiny compared to his size.

News travelled quickly that Kyawaleta had killed many men in the night. The mass killing had affected the remaining men, women and children of the tribe who chose to flee to settle in a different location. Nii, his younger brother Koembo along with Pyapowa now lived on the abandoned land. Lengame would eventually marry and join Nii here.

Life in their new settlement moved peacefully until Pyapowa's father and elder brother were killed in a tribal fight with the neighbouring tribe. Word that this enemy tribe was preparing a Moka with the Traleya tribe reached Nii. He gathered his tribesmen around him to plan a retaliation attack during the Moka ceremony. Plans were kept secret so no word reached their enemy.

The brothers prepared themselves according to Moka customs. A pig was roasted because it was believed that the spirits of the dead demanded it. In the process of roasting it, they were required to pray to the spirits of their dead relatives and ancestors to give them strength and courage. They prayed to the spirits:

> *"Our ancestors have power*
>
> *Our relatives have strength*
>
> *Grant us your power and strength tomorrow,*
>
> *So that our enemies may not kill us as they killed you all.*
>
> *May we be protected from our enemies;*
>
> *Come and be in our weapons*
>
> *So that we may shoot to kill.*
>
> *If you will help us to kill,*

Then let the skull of the pig's head be

Smashed into pieces in the roasting pit.

But if we will not kill any men,

What we are hoping that should happen must not.

If it does not happen we will not go and attack".

While the pork meat was in the roasting pit, Pyapowa approached Nii and Koembo and asked, "If you two do not mind, can I go and spy at the Moka place to see if the enemies had come to sleep there."

The brothers responded.

"Sure, you may go but watch out for enemies."

He quickly ran down the bush tracks along the Mount Hagen range and hid behind the bushes. Very carefully he looked and saw the leader of the enemy tribe sitting with the other men.

Pyapowa returned to his tribe and was asked by Nii, "Brother did you see any man of the rival tribe?"

"Yes, I saw Pombra Kit, the leader of the rival tribe, sitting with some other men but I doubt whether we will kill them because they are big" Pyapowa replied.

"He is there today but I am sure he will go home tomorrow. Do not be upset or discouraged. We will take out the pig we roasted and tell from the skull whether we will be successful or not", Nii assured them.

They removed the roasted pork meat from the pit. Cheering broke out when they discovered that the head was smashed into pieces. Nii exclaimed "you see what happened; tomorrow we will surely kill more of our enemies."

Excitement that they would be successful in killing some of their enemies settled over the men as they ate some of the meat, packing away the rest for the next day. As darkness fell, they finally slept.

At dawn the next morning, the warriors prepared for their battle then departed, walking very cautiously and watchfully carrying their axes, spears, bows and arrows. As they approached the village where the enemies stayed, a tall, well-built man walked out of the house. Pombra Kit, the leader of the enemy tribe and bare handed, ran into the pit toilet. Nii quietly ran to the toilet and stood at the entrance. Pombra Kit was very tall so when he exited the toilet he bent down, his head appearing first. Nii wasted no time. He lifted his stone axe, landed it heavily on Pombra Kit's neck and chopped off his head. Immediately Nii and his tribesmen quickly and quietly ran way without being noticed.

War cries broke the stillness of the forest when the tribesmen of Pombra Kit learnt that he had been killed. Full-scale tribal war broke out between both tribes. During the fierce battle Pyapowa received an arrow wound below his right eye that eventually healed, his fellow warriors not seriously injured at all. Their enemies were killed.

CHAPTER 2

HIS BRIDE LENGAME

When Nii recovered from his fighting he again visited with Lengame. When the elders from Lengame's tribe saw that she continuously had courtship with Nii, they deduced that Nii was interested in Lengame.

Since marriage at that time was not done through love but through societies and clan interests, the elders of the Senapun tribe where Lengame comes from decided that she would marry Nii. They were also of the view that once Lengame married Nii, he would become a shield protecting their tribe from enemies. Both Nii and Lengame's tribes agreed that the couple would marry by virtue of the prevailing custom in the two clans. A decision that the bride price ceremony would be staged at Nii's parent's village, Kimalipe, some twenty kilometres from Kuipboat, overlooking Enga province was reached.

Talk between the villagers was that Nii would marry Lengame. Then on a sunny morning, calls and kundu drums signalled the entire neighbouring villages that something special was going to happen.

Lengame, dressed fully in her traditional attire, was escorted by several female members of her clan to Nii's house where Nii's family welcomed her. The ceremony took place immediately.

Laik Tekepe, Nii's father, together with other members of the family of the Kyakini tribe dressed in their custom finery, laid out a container full of crude oil extracted from tree trunks, 12 live pigs, 2 cassowaries, 12 pig husks and 22 bundles of kina shells (shell from the sea) in front of the bride's family.

After examining the goods, they acknowledged their acceptance of the bride price payment.

Lengame was a brave woman and very pretty. Everyone talked about her. She had fled to her family's home after her first marriage ended due to the death of her husband during tribal conflict. She had taken on traditional roles and was busy doing gardening, and looking after the pigs for her parents. Her personal demeanour and kind attitude towards other people drew positive comments from the nearby societies. Many parents were keen to gain Lengame as a wife for their sons.

In contrast, Nii was a fierce warrior who won bitter wars against several clans. People feared that if there were tribal conflict between their clan and Nii's clan, Nii would chase them and chop off their heads. So they were subservient and kind, seeking to be friends with him.

After the bride price ceremony, Lengame was left behind with Nii's family. Everyone else including her relatives went back to their own villages. Nii's family offered a big feast with several pig killings to officially accept Lengame into the family, to initiate Nii into manhood.

CHAPTER 3

ANCESTORS

I am Lengame's grandchild, Paul Puri Nii. As I sat at her feet as a young child, she filled my mind with her stories of the early days of our tribe.

The spirits of the dead and the fear-provoking war cries by the warriors in the middle of the night frightened the people of the South as they sat in the cave around their fireplace. At that time of the night, these men occasionally poked their heads out of the cave's entrance to grasp a clear view of the world beyond, a world far beyond their imagination. They pretended to sit courageously next to each other, comforted their bare bodies with their hands, made more fires, nervously laughed and boasted about their ancestors' successful hunting trips. Yet the fear of the outside world still troubled them.

Mothers forced their nipples into their infants' mouths to stop them from crying or making any sound.

The giant prickly and spiny insects continued to move noisily around searching for food as the anxious men begged for the dawn to overcome the fear. It seemed the sun would never rise. Then a different sound of insect singing was heard as morning dawned, indicating the sun would rise soon on the horizon. As the crowned pigeon and colourful parrots joined the early morning birds' chorus, the Southerners fell into a comfortable sleep leaving their memories of the bad night behind.

Not all Southern warriors slept.

One had ventured out hunting alone in the thick forest. He piggy-backed his catch, a wild boar together with some wild fowl and stood at the entrance to the cave. The nearby forest was still covered with morning fog as he turned to face the cave again. Not a soul raised their head to congratulate him on his successful hunting trip. In his disenchantment, he left all his catch near the cave and went to the hillside on the northern end of the cave where they had their gardens. He collected greens and other vegetables to be roasted together with the boar he had killed.

His expectation that his cave people would appreciate his hunting skills and help with the preparation of the feast was not met. Upon arrival at the cave, the people were awake but their minds were still carried away by the strange thing that happened during the night. They showed little interest in his feast but he continued with his task. He shared the roasted meat and all enjoyed the big feed. As dusk began to settle all the men and their wives and young ones moved into the cave in preparation for the night's sleep.

Except for the warrior. He moved past the dying embers of the fire to stand at the cave's entrance easily observing the men of the South holding their wives firmly with their palms while comfortably crisscrossing their legs over each other as they drifted off to sleep. The warrior was very upset at how his men of South had behaved; men who had no intentions of bravery but chose to spend most of their time with their wives. He thought that those men's territory was vulnerable to attack by the enemies. His frustration overwhelmed him till he decided to flee the valley of the South leaving the cowards behind before enemies attacked them.

He never told anyone about his intentions to leave the valley.

During that night, he quickly grabbed hold of his bows and arrows and headed north, walking uphill for hours until he came to a summit where he rested on a rock to relieve his tired body. After a short rest and a move to begin his journey again, he turned his head around to have a last glimpse of his beautiful valley of the

South. He could not believe his eyes as he sighted sparkling fires everywhere over the valley and sadly assumed that it was his valley that had been attacked by enemies.

Filled with discontented thoughts, he continued to follow a small track in the jungle until he reached a small creek. At the bank of the river, he lay down for a rest until it was daybreak.

Not knowing what to do, the poor warrior kept on following the creek stopping to eat the wild birds and cassowary that he killed. Up the hills, down the valleys, tirelessly continued his journey for weeks and months until he reached a beautiful place. As he looked around he saw a haze of smoke in the distance so he moved onwards. A newly built garden stood on his path. He was easily convinced that spirits of the forest could not make gardens, so it was an indication of a sign of human beings. He was not wrong with his thinking. Not far from him stood an old couple who seemed surprised by his appearance and started communicating with him in a language he could not understand. With sign language the couple invited the warrior to follow them to their house.

The couple lived alone with their young daughter in this new land the warrior had found and they invited the warrior to stay with them for some time. As he learned their language, he discovered that the couple had been waiting for a warrior to marry their daughter and inherit their kingdom. It seemed the old man's kingdom stretched across the forest forever. It seemed also that the warrior was responsive to the idea but more so to marrying the young daughter he had become emotionally involved with than managing a kingdom.

As time passed, the old couple died. The daughter and the warrior lived happily in the forest with lots to eat. Their first son Kyakini was born followed by a second son Troepo three years later. Their father taught them how to become hunters and gathers, at times returning home from hunting with wild boar and cassowaries.

The time came for the sons to seek their own territories, conquering forests and each setting up their own compound. Kyakini married four young women, building each a house spread over four corners of the new territory. He raised many children who grew to be skillful hunters, as well as gathering wives along the way.

Many children were born, all growing up to practice polygamy as the way of their culture.

Troepo, Kyakini's younger brother married five women who produced many children also growing up to practice polygamy.

The brothers gave their names to the two tribes who currently cover the Baiyer area of Western Highlands Province of New Guinea.

It had been a long morning so my grandmother and I moved to her kitchen to find food for lunch. I loved my grandmother and clung to her stories that she told with so much warmth and knowingness. After lunch we moved to our special place and she continued with the history of our people.

Several generations later, Ehepunge, a descendant of Kyakini, settled at Kimalipe, a village hundreds of kilometers away from Kuipboat. He was tall, well built and strong with a reputation for grabbing and killing tree pythons while showing no fear with animals that cowed others. A skillful hunter and a fierce warrior, Ehepunge was accorded shelter, food and respect wherever he went. He conquered most of the unclaimed territories near Kimalipe frightening off the neighbouring tribes who lived nearby; who disappeared into the thick jungles to escape any possible attack by the warrior. Ehepunge was the protector of his tribe and his tribesmen and women felt safe around him. His words on any community affairs were final and nobody disputed it. He was their godfather.

Ehepunge was also a womaniser and polygamous. He married 50 women, plus mistresses were spread across the neighbouring tribes. He began to lose favour with his tribesmen because he often never married his wives properly, made many pregnant and abandoned them. There were no complaints from his wives as they feared their husband would come and chop their heads off with his stone axe.

Of all the wives he had, his last wife gave birth to a son named Tekepe. But Ehepunge did not see his son grow up to be a warrior. Food poisoning took Ehepunge's life leaving his poor wife to raise the child by herself.

Tekepe was a great warrior and a hunter but he was not a womaniser like his father. He married only one wife and was a well-respected leader of the Kyakini people settled at Kimalipe. Unlike his father, he spoke of peace and harmony wanting his tribe to enjoy happiness at all times. He possessed extraordinary charisma that attracted the entire community. A charismatic leader, he died of old age.

He left behind him several daughters and two sons. His last son was named Laik. By the time Laik was ready to settle as an adult, the village of Kimalipe was so over-crowded he had to explore other options. Enemy tribes were established in the territory he considered suitable for his future. War was necessary to capture new ground. With support from his tribesmen Laik attacked. Large numbers of the enemy were killed while those left standing chose to move to the far north of the country.

Laik settled peacefully at Marlama, married a young woman from a neighbouring tribe and had a lot of daughters but he needed a son to inherit his legacy. The inability to breed a son was a constant worry so much so he approached the chief of the Troepo tribe.

Believed to be half human and half spirit due to his foretelling of the future and his miraculous happenings, the Troepo chief listened carefully to Laik's dilemma.

Since the Troepo and the Kyakini tribes had originated from two brothers, the chief told him that he would attend to his problem and in that he assured him not to be troubled at all.

"Your wife can not give birth to a male child because your wife's ancestors had originated from the enemy tribe. Spells not to bear a male offspring have been cast on your wife by those from whose tribe you have killed. Go back home, kill a big pig and make feast on it. Before you eat the meat, call out the names of your fore fathers who died some generations ago. Ask them to chase away the spell that has been caste on your wife. Then you must wait two weeks before sleeping with your wife".

Laik followed the advice once back at home. Some months later his wife was pregnant. A baby boy was born and named Nii. A second son followed a year later given the name Koembo. Both boys learned the art of the warrior and had reached their adult prime years when their parents both passed away at an old age.

This was the Nii I married".

I returned to my home that had been built next to my grandmother, Lengame's house lost in the stories of my tribal ancestors.

CHAPTER 4

PARAKA'S BIRTH

One of my favourite relatives is my Uncle Paraka Nii, the first born of seven sons of my grandparents, Lengame and Nii. My father Puri was their second child.

Lengame often told Paraka that before he was born she had a baby boy who died at birth. It was assumed by Nii that the unsatisfied spirits had caused the tragic death of this innocent little baby. As a great warrior, Nii had killed so many men in both open battle and in covert attacks. Consequently, he believed the spirits of those men whom he killed harmed his family members whenever there was an opportunity. The death of this baby boy sat heavily on his mind. In such situations, society required the individual concerned to make sacrifices to the spirits before or after the birth of a child. Sacrifices were done in the form of a pig killing or finding a magician to chase the evil spirits away from coming close to the pregnant mothers. Nii had failed miserably to do either of those, feeling full of regret that he had ignored his culture that had existed for generations. When Lengame conceived with her next baby, Nii was diligent in his approach for assistance.

He looked for the magician named Yakka from the Troepo Yawea tribe. The Troepo and Kyakini tribes originated from a common ancestor therefore men of these two tribes did not intermarry. They helped each other both in times of trouble and need, especially during times of tribal fighting.

Yakka lived behind the mountains, some kilometres away at Koyagamanda, a place where Nii spent some of his childhood. Prior to his departure, Nii explained his plans to Lengame who lovingly gave her support. On the day of the journey Nii left before sunrise. He had thick forests to walk through, steep mountains to climb and fast rivers to cross. He reached his destination just after the sun was directly overhead.

From a distance the magician watched with surprise as Nii walked towards his house.

"It seems today will a fine day for you isn't it, Mr. Nii?" was the magician's warm greeting, a statement used to greet someone who is a very close friend. They shook hands having not seen each other for years and fell into deep conversation discussing issues that were of great concern to them both. Eventually, Yakka asked Mr. Nii, "is there anything in particular that you came to see me about?"

"Yes," Nii replied. "I came to see you about the cause of the death of my first-born son. We are so worried our child was a very healthy baby but died mysteriously."

Yakka listened attentively as Nii told him the story.

"We believe the spirits of the dead have killed him so I came to talk to you about it so that you could chase the spirits away from my wife. I do not want the same thing to happen to our baby about to be born."

After listening to the sad story the magician kindly offered to help.

"Before I do anything, you must perform a certain task in order for what I will do for you to work.

You must pay careful attention to what I will tell you to do and you must do so accordingly."

Nii listened carefully.

"What will happen if I do not follow your orders?"

"If you do not follow my instructions and do something else instead, then what I will do for you will not work."

Yakka proceeded with his instructions.

"You are to climb down a very steep hill. And then when you are at the foot of the hill you will see a creek in which you are to fetch water from the direction the water flowed and not against it as is usually the case. While you bend down to fetch water you must listen carefully for any sound that may be made by animals. If you hear a bird's sound, your wife will have a son; however, the opposite will happen if you hear the noise of a frog."

Feeling a bit reluctant after the tiring journey, Nii picked up a stalk of hollowed bamboo that was leaning against the wall outside the house, left Yakka and started climbing down the steep hill towards the creek. Finally he arrived at the creek and prepared to fetch water. With high expectations of a boy, Nii listened attentively to capture a single noise that any animal could make while fetching the water. Not a single noise was heard until the bamboo stalk was half-filled; an aliyo bird sat right above him on a tree branch and started singing. It was the happiest moment of Nii's life as he knew his hopes of a son would soon be realised.

Nii was overwhelmed with excitement at the sign that he had witnessed. At the same time he was frightened by the strange noises that the bird made. However the excitement overcame the fear and he bravely fetched the water and started climbing the steep hill towards the magician's home. By the time he had arrived at Yakka's house it was already late for him to go back to his home.

After he had rested for a while Yakka asked him, "Did anything happen like I said it would while you were fetching water?"

"Yes," Nii responded.

"An aliyo sat on a dry branch just above where I was fetching water and sang very frightening songs." Nii told the magician.

"Do not worry because it was a sign that your wife will bear you a son who will be a great man in future." Yakka reassured the father-to-be.

The magician got the bamboo stalk of water from Nii and held it in his right hand. While Nii watched Yakka closed his eyes and meditated upon it. He said some words in a strange language that Nii could not interpret. After the meditation he handed the bamboo stalk containing the water to Nii to take home and reaffirmed "Nii, my brother, things will be all right so do not worry over the spirits anymore."

Nii thanked Yakka enthusiastically and left for home carrying the bamboo stack of water. As dusk fell he was only mid-way through his journey so it was late at night when he arrived home. Lengame was still awake, so Nii shared his experience with his wife. He then asked her to drink the water he had carried in the bamboo stalk. She did. A few months later Paraka was born at the Maralama village, the home of my grandparents at that time.

The year was 1939. It was a time where nothing was known about the existence of the outside world. It would be eight more years before the first white men arrived in the Western Highlands. Even though life seemed primitive during those times, my people experienced very interesting days and nights.

Naming of babies during those primitive eras was based on predictions about the child's future fame in terms of wealth and chieftain roles. My grandmother told me that Nii named their first son Lome, a name signifying a superior male who could stand like a fence to keep enemies away from attacking one's territory. Nii was certain his son would be a great warrior, a shield protecting the whole of the Kyakini tribe.

It was only a few days after his birth that the baby Lome had his name changed to Paraka. His maternal uncle, Gaiyer Kumba heard of the baby's birth so he came to visit. He carried with him a recent story that had impressed him enormously. A man by the name of Paraka from the Trolakae tribe had killed two brothers from the Jepinji tribe of the Western Highlands Province at the same time.

His only weapon one spear. Once Paraka had killed one brother he pushed the other brother over and cut his neck using his teeth. The man died.

Mr Kumba thought that the baby Lome would be a tough warrior like that big warrior Paraka of the Trolakae tribe. He encouraged Lengame and Nii to change the baby's name to Paraka. Because the bird of paradise was also called Paraka in the Kyaka language of the Baiyer River society, Lengame thought it would be an appropriate name for her son. The bird of paradise is unique and colourful, confirming her thoughts that Paraka would one day be a unique leader with colourful characteristics. Despite little or even no Christian doctrines, Lengame believed that there was an invisible God that existed, a creator, and that through him life was sustained. This was a God who monitored the law of nature and one who knew the future of the babies. She prayed to the God saying:

"Thank you for my son, my God

May you make him grow strong and almighty

So that he will grow up to be a great man.

Make him to become a wealthy man in future

In with pigs, kina shells, crude oil.

Make him become an example of a better leader,

A common figure to the people of the Kyakini Tribe and the Baiyer society as a whole."

When Lengame told Paraka about her prayer years later, he was fascinated to hear that even before the white man arrived in her territory she believed in the God that the present Christians preached.

"Our actions, thoughts and behaviour have been preplanned by the Lord our God at the very time when we were first conceived", she told her son.

Paraka was guided by his God loving mother but also spent just as much time as a toddler with his Uncle Gaiyer spending a week or two in his presence. The little boy loved being carried on his uncle's shoulders, singing together as they went to find suitable land to make new gardens. When his uncle found beetles in the woods he would cook them, handing the hot beetles to Paraka to eat. As he sat eating the tiny beetles, he would sing this song in his tribal language:

"Pai– a – pa – wae – a - ----

Rakan kuke dupa nao pisaro lyse

Rakan epenge dupwa popo penyale."

Translation: "Father, I will eat the small ones first while the big ones are cooling down."

Uncle Gaiyer showered Paraka with love but also with discipline. The young Paraka learned quickly not to upset his uncle who acted more as a father in their interactions.

Tribal warfare in most parts of our society was a way of life when Paraka was a small boy. His mother would carefully watch and guide her young child to keep him safe. But he did not miss the telling of the story of his Uncle Pyapowa's master plan to kill his rival chief. Sitting quietly under the shade of the big klinki pine tree, Paraka heard the adults talking.

"My plan at first was to slowly chop down a tree waiting till my enemy appeared and with the final whack, allow the tree to fall and kill the enemy target. Then I decided to use my rival's wife to poison her husband, said Pyapowa.

While I was chopping at the tree I noticed the wife approach. I felt a little anxious but I greeted the lady with a smile. She returned my smile and said to me:

"Good morning Pyapowa, the day seems pleasant today, isn't it?"

"Yes, it certainly is a fine day today," Pyapowa agreed.

"Why are you chopping the tree?" the lady questioned him.

"I am just trying to extract timbers from it to build a house," explained Pyapowa.

"Okay, you go on, I am going to the garden to gather some food" she said.

"I don't think I will finish this job so I will still be here when you come back from the garden," Pyapowa replied.

Day after day the lady moved to the garden and back home. Pyapowa was slowly chopping, splitting and doing all that he was supposed to do with his blunt stone axe. Several times he brought cooked food to eat when he was hungry and to share with the lady when returning from her gardens. Sugarcane was a staple food along with kaukau, aibika, pitpit and other raw food.

On the day he followed his usual routine, Pyapowa took sugarcane but this time he carried a poison that makes people go insane. Iiwaliwa makes those who take it reveal secrets and kill immediate relatives when asked to do so by the person who gives the poison.``

The sky was grey with clouds building on the horizon as the unsuspecting lady returned from her work at the garden. Pyapowa saw her coming towards him quickly: spreading some of the liwaliwa on the sugarcane that he kept aside for her. As she drew closer, he greeted her and offered her the poisoned sugarcane. She thanked him, chewed it and headed home. Pyapowa went to his home.

Once at home Pyapowa mixed a heavier does of poison to give it to the lady so that she could kill her husband. In the meantime, the lady was beginning to feel the effects of the liwaliwa.

She found herself feeling deeply sorry for Pyapowa for no reason. When she saw her poisoner the next day she yelled at him:

"If you ask me to do anything for you, even if it is the worst, I will surely do it for you,"

Pyapowa remained quiet for a while. Then after a few minutes he looked at her and asked, 'If I asked you would be willing to kill your husband with a poison"?

Intoxicated with the poison from the previous day, the lady did not hesitate with her answer. "Sure I'll do that. Where is the poison, show it to me." she demanded.

Pyapowa handed the poison to her with the following instructions.

"You must kill him with it as soon as you go home and on the next day you are to come back to meet me here. Once he has eaten the poisoned food you must go outside and make a big fire, I will stay here and watch. If I see smoke rising up I will know that you have poisoned him."

The lady answered in an obedient tone.

"I certainly am going to do as you ask. He normally eats at my house and not at his other wives' houses so there is no doubt that I will kill him."

Driven by the effects of the Iiwaliwa poison, the lady quickly and carefully prepared a delicious meal composed of pitpit, greens and api saltand including other staple food such as kaukau and sugarcane. Her husband entered the house as usual for his evening meal unaware that his wife was smothering his food with poison so powerful that it kills people a few hours after they have taken it. The husband retired to his bed but never woke up.

As the morning fog cleared, the lady made a huge fire outside her house producing an enormous amount of smoke. When Pyapowa saw the smoke he started singing. He removed an armband that he had worn since his elder brother and father were killed in a tribal fight. When Nii saw his cousin removing his armband and singing, he knew right away that Pyapowa had taken revenge over the earlier slaughter of his late brother and father. Revenge had been taken.

Pyapowa then cut sugarcane near his house and took it for the lady when he went to meet her. In his bag, was another kind of liwaliwa that cures people from the previous one. Pyapowa's aim was to give the second *liwaliwa to the lady so that she was back to her conscious, the way she was before she took the liwaliwa. Otherwise, she would reveal to others the secret that she had poisoned her own husband.*

The two met as planned. Pyapowa asked the lady if she had really killed her husband. "I poisoned him yesterday, he is a dead man, why are you so worried?" the lady replied. "Thank you so much, I'm so glad you did," Pyapowa said.

He gave her the sugarcane that he had smeared with the poison liwaliwa. Remember, this kind of liwaliwa was meant to heal the lady from the changed state of mind caused by the previous liwaliwa. She chewed the sugarcane and became sober. By then she realised that she had killed her own husband and was very upset. On the other hand, she would not reveal that she was asked to poison him because she did not want to put Pyapowa, Nii and Koembo and the rest of the tribe into trouble. The husband of the lady died while they were talking. Pyapowa promised the lady that he would reward her for the desire she fulfilled after her husband's funeral. They bid each other farewell and separated to their homes.

CHAPTER 5

CHILDHOOD ON THE MOUNTAINS

Paraka grew up as a child at Maralama village. As an older brother, he always treated his six younger brothers and sisters the way his parents related to their children. His watchful and caring attitude to others was learned at the feet of his parents, unlike those of some other children around his same age.

Paraka's father did not live with them in the family house but lived in the men's house known as hausman or "akalianda" due to the long-held customary beliefs in most parts of Highlands society that men were not supposed to live with their wives or any other women except at certain times. The women and children lived in the women's house (hausmeri). They did not miss their father because he always came to visit them to help the mothers with the vegetable gardening and other jobs that needed his attention

Agriculture was central to the lifestyles of the highland tribes. Paraka's family gardens were situated at a place called Tramalo where they went very early in the mornings to work tilling the soil and tending their food supply. It was often very chilly and frosty in the mornings so at times their mothers were reluctant to wake the children from their sleep. If any stayed behind, they would arrive later with their father once the sun had warmed the morning. If a parent found strong reluctance to get up for their gardening chores, a mention of participating in some of their hobbies, such as killing rats, grasshoppers and so forth got the desired result.

As a little one Paraka was able to walk long distances while his other brothers and sisters struggled with walking, their parents would piggyback them. The moment they reached the gardens, Paraka led the little children to the small bushes to trap rats. Rat killing was one of their favourite hobbies they enjoyed very much.

Their father had taught them to search for holes in the earth and reminded them that if they noticed one to call him so that he would kill the rats for them. The urge to prove their ability to kill ran strongly through their veins so there was always the attempt to kill at least one rat before calling their father.

The rats were often very clever by fooling the youngsters by escaping through other holes. For those rats not so clever they were killed with spears and Paraka's father never missed. He was always successful. Rats were edible in those times so they piled them up and their father made big mumu as they were helpless. At other times he would kill a pig or two for them as a substitute for rats. The youngsters also loved catching grasshoppers turning it into a competition to see who could catch the most.

When the work in the gardens was finished Paraka's mothers would carry the huge bilums filled with food, mainly Highland sweet potatoes (kaukau), cassava, pitpit, banana and all sorts of locally grown food. Since, Paraka was the eldest; he used to help his mothers by at least carrying a bit of the food in a small bilum. Although the bilums were heavy, his mother used to carry one of the three younger children, either Napil, Puri or Tiptip in their bags on top of the food bilums. His father Nii carried the other children.

The food garden was located in the valley and as such, it was very difficult walking uphill to their home especially with the heavy loads. They did not need to gather firewood because there was a surplus on the mountains around where they lived. The stream was far from their home so they travelled long distances to fetch water to drink but not for cooking because they did not have any pots during those times.

Nii had taken a second wife called Dawe from the Ukuni *Kagleme* tribe who lived not far from the wide and long eared people. During that time, Paraka's Kyakini tribe had good relationships with the Kagleme and their neighbouring Depints tribe. They had common interests in terms of the Moka ceremony, marriage, pig killing and accumulated other customary wealth items. It was through one of those ceremonial occasions that paved way for Nii to marry Dawe. Nii's younger brother, Koembo, also found one of his wives from the Depints tribe. Inter marriage between the tribes of Kagleme, Depints and Kyakini were so common and continue even today.

Unlike Paraka's current five wives who quarrel over little things, his mother Lengame and stepmother Dawe were very friendly, loving and co-operative. They always went together to either of their places whenever there was a harvest or feast. Paraka was close to his stepsister Napil, the eldest daughter of his stepmother Dawe. When asked to go fetch water, both Paraka and Napil would respond quickly grabbing for the stalks of hollowed bamboos running along the zigzagged track that lead to the stream.

The children made their own fun hunting down rats, chasing butterflies, grasshoppers, caterpillars, locusts and many other insects. Paraka joined other boys his own age, Peyapenge, Kiap, Raima and Lasi, hunting with their bows and arrows specifically made for each of them. Paraka's father crafted bows and the sharpest arrows for his son so that he could kill many rats. At times he could gather up to twenty rats that impressed the younger children who giggled and danced around in their excitement at his success. The older girls collected wild greens such as ferns and 'kun' kun, to be roasted with the rats while the youngest children went fossicking insects in a different area.

Paraka was fast in preparing the rats for a meal. His father had taught him well. Their intestines were removed in a similar manner to how pigs were prepared for cooking. A pit was dug and a fire lit in it. Stones were spread on top to heat up. The meal's meat, pig or rat, was lowered onto the stones, covered and left to cook slowly. When the mumu or, rock oven, was ready, banana leaves were spread along the ground in a straight line. A medium-sized stick was poked into the ground alongside the leaves indicating the number of children present to eat.

The preparation of the mumu and sharing were done in the manner of a feast. But before the children were given their share of food someone had to give a brief speech. Most of the young ones were not confident to talk publicly but Paraka showed no sign of embarrassment or shyness. He spoke easily in front of the clan and made sure all the children were well fed before commencing his own meal.

Paraka's parents isolated their children from the rest of the Kyakini tribe members as well as other people to ensure that their enemies could not kidnap or kill them. His father Nii was the leader and great warrior of their tribe with enemies keen to kill him. The children came out only for special occasions such as moka, feast or singsing, always accompanied by their parents. Lessons were taught not to accept any food from a stranger, to eat only food from their blood and immediate relatives. Nii was clever enough to avoid poison and even attacks from his enemies often telling his own boys, Puri, Tiptip and Paraka, "you boys are going to be leaders like me in future. So listen to me and do not go to places that I do not want you all to go. If you refuse and go anywhere on your own and get killed then nobody will become a leader in my place when I die."

Paraka's brothers and sisters did not always hang around with other children but sometimes helped their parents to do various chores in and around the house, breaking firewood and fetching water. Sometimes they were told to spend their day at the pig sty either to keep other pigs out of their territory or to keep their own pigs in so that they did not go out and destroyed other people's property, such as gardens. They were very obedient and their parents admired them a lot and often impressed on the sons that they would be good future leaders.

The *Senapuni* and the Ukuni Kalgme tribes were not enemies so Nii would let his boys visit their various uncles' places to plant and harvest food crops or even bring some spare pork meat left over from a feast back to their own home.

When the mothers were away the children would do little chores knowing that they would be rewarded with the best part of the meat from the feast or moka, they performed those tasks willingly. Only positive comments were heard repeatedly from the children's parents. They told them that they were good, obedient, honest and kind children and other people would admire them. "You are all very nice children, keep up these deeds so that not only we would love you but other people will like you too."

As an elder child in the family Paraka firmly followed directions and led by example. Whenever he had food, he always shared with others inviting people as they strolled by to come into his house to eat. Such qualities he possessed were partly from his parents' guidance but some were naturally acquired. As Tiptip, Napil, Puri and Paraka grew older there were other children born into the family of both mothers. The four eldest children acted most responsibly, doing most of the household jobs while looking after their younger brothers and sisters while their parents were away working in the gardens.

As he grew older he developed acts of cunning to impress his parents. When his mother asked him to go and get some water he pretended that he did not hear what she said, quietly moving out of the house with the hollowed bamboo trunks that were used to fetch water. He would quickly run to the creek and get some water then run back hiding the trunks outside. He would then go into the house where his mother asked him "did you go and get some water as I told you to?" He answered that he had not so she angrily asked him again to go and fetch water. He quickly ran over to where he hid the water containers and brought them in to the house in just a few minutes surprising his mother because the stream was far away. She had never expected him to return so quickly so both his parents were pleased and heaped praise on his ability.

A few months later while his own mother was absent, Paraka took a piglet from its mother and hid it in a cave-like hole in the ground. The hole was dug alongside a big drain that his father had dug to keep their pigs from destroying other people's gardens on the mountains. Paraka made it impossible for the pig to escape by closing the hole with wood.

Paraka fed the piglet with pitpit, cooked sweet potatoes, soft kaukau leaves and a bit of his meals. He also sucked sugarcane juice and fed the piglet with it and made sure that no one noticed what he did. His mother always counted the number of piglets at birth and on the day she realised one was missing, she began searching everywhere. Paraka pretended that he knew nothing about it. After seeing no sign of the piglet his mother gave up because she thought it could have died and was eaten by other pigs.

After three or four months had passed Paraka said to his mother, "I saw something and am so scared to go close to it. Come with me and you will see it. There it is, look inside." His mother was frightened in case it was a snake but Paraka insisted that she should look inside. By then the piglet had already grown bigger and healthier than those that were left with the mothers. The moment she looked in her eyes grasped the figure of a piglet and she could not believe it until he confirmed that it was the piglet that she had been searching for everywhere. She hugged him and said to him "when you grow up you will be a big man in terms of marrying many wives, having many pigs and becoming a leader."

He acknowledges today that what she said had come to fruition. He has five wives with twenty-five children, twenty-seven grand children and a great-grand child. He is a distinguished leader and has much wealth in terms of leadership qualities and pig killings.

CHAPTER 6

ARRIVAL OF THE WHITE MEN

A call echoed across the cold and misty air one early morning. It was very similar to the call made when enemies mounted a surprise attack on a clan or tribe. Paraka was only eight years old and was easily overwhelmed with fear at times when he heard such calls. He would quickly fold his legs and try to go to sleep.

This morning Nii was outside the house with his bow and arrows as soon as he had heard the call. There was a better chance to escape when enemies attacked if one was outside the house rather than inside. He returned to the house and said, "the strange men are on their way."

Rumours had spread earlier throughout the clan that two white-skinned cannibals were settling at Ogelbeng a few kilometres north of Mount Hagen. Strange, frightening and funny things were told about those two white cannibals. These strangers carried a stick-like object that could kill pigs, dogs, birds and even human beings with a loud noise in a split second. Everybody feared these two strange men after having heard all the rumours about them. Now they were on their way to Baiyer River and Paraka's tribesmen did not know what to do. They planned to kill the two cannibals. However, when they arrived they were accompanied by men from the Jika tribe from around Mount Hagen. Since Nii's men had a good relationship with the men of Jika the white cannibals lived to see another day.

The white men came to Baiyer and first settled at Trolga, a village situated at the foot of the Mount Hagen range and beside the Baiyer valley. They built a big tent when viewed from Maralama, Paraka's village that matched the color of the sky. Therefore the people of Baiyer said the white men had built a, "yakianda (Heaven house)," for themselves. His parents restricted Paraka and the other children from going close to the tent because they thought the house would swallow them. Some adults were also frightened of going near the white men and their tent.

Eventually, a few people started approaching these strange men and were given gifts of salt, soap, mirror and axes. Gradually more and more moved towards the white men with high expectations of gifts. As they learned these intruders were not cannibals they lost their fear and began to trade foodstuff for gifts.

Paraka's mother Lengame regularly visited the white men. When she returned with a white object Paraka was excited and interested. She told him this was called soap that could easily remove the dirt on his body to be used with water. Paraka got the thing from his mother's bag and held it in his hands. He had never smelt such a lovely smell before. Heavy rain was falling so his mother allowed him to take the soap and bathe in the rain with it. Dripping wet, he rubbed it all over his body producing bubbles that got into his eyes and hurt. Paraka thought he would become blind for life so he ran all the way to a nearby creek where he washed all the bubbles off his body and rinsed his eyes. It was even said that if they washed their bodies everyday with soap the colour of their skins would change to the white men's colour.

Paraka wanted to be like the white men so he washed with soap daily, however his skin never changed. Later he was told that the white men were born white and had not changed to white by showering daily with soap. He then realised how silly he was and stopped having showers regularly like he used to.

He still admired the white men and wanted to be like them because he thought they were superior to the blacks. He was much older when he learnt they were all equal. The difference was that the white men had been civilised earlier.

The day his mother returned home from her visit to the white men carrying some white grain wrapped in a piece of cloth, Paraka touched and examined this strange new object. They looked exactly like the eggs of ants but to his surprise they felt so strong unlike the ants' eggs.

His mother put the grains into a hollowed bamboo and poured some water into it, carefully closing the mouth of the bamboo and placed it in the flames of the fire to be cooked. She attended to it for some minutes and then took it out of the fire after it was cooked. It tasted like kaukau when they ate it but smelt different. Paraka had tasted his first meal of plain white rice.

More than a year had passed as the family adjusted to the white men in their midst, Paraka was now nine years old when they were told that there was another group of white men coming, men more fierce looking than the earlier ones. They were known as patrol officers or kiaps.

Men from other tribes where the patrol officers had passed through their village also came, helping to carry the patrol boxes. It was common knowledge in Paraka's society during those early days that a man who took turns in carrying the patrol officer's boxes was superior to others. He was feared and respected by the rest of the members of the community. As a result, most of the young men who carried boxes earned so much praise and gained popularity in the society. When one of the box carriers stood up to say something, everyone would say, "he is closer to the kiaps so let us hear what he's got to say." Paraka too respected and feared the men who were closer to the white men.

During that time, Paraka's parents were still living up at their village, Maralama and sometimes when Paraka looked down the Baiyer valley, he could see people moving in single lines. There were no trees like there is today but only grassland so he had a clear view of the men carrying boxes and other properties that belonged to the patrol officers. The carriers were so proud and they made themselves obvious by singing songs as they were walking from the village-to-village or visiting different clans and tribes.

The people of Baiyer called the white men Mata Kae, Mata Rapia, Mata Joe and Moa. Paraka thought these were nicknames. However, Mata or Master was a common word normally used to address all the white men.

The patrol officers once settled found that they needed some natives to work with them as translators between themselves and the rest of the native population to communicate effectively. The patrol officers appointed young men to act as their immediate agents in each tribe and they called them Bos bois. Some of those included Kumbwao-Maip tribe and Rapi-Romba of the Ukuni Rapi and Kongrui, the stepbrother of Paraka's cousin Raima therefore Kongrui had a good relationship with Paraka and his family.

Kongrui was a very fierce and strict person. When people did not follow his instructions, he commanded them to lift one of their legs up and he hit them very hard with his cane stick. Some people pissed when they were hit with the cane. When he came around to visit they said, "Kongrui one leg up is coming," an expression that referred to him.

Nii's younger brother Koembo was also appointed as the bosboi of their Kyakini tribe. He was also very hard and cruel like the others when he meant business. He hit anybody including his relatives with his cane stick.

In those days, there were so many things that needed to be done. The Australian Administrators, farmers and missionaries needed roads so building of roads was very common everywhere. The tribes living between Baiyer River and Hagen were working very hard to build a road with nothing but their hands. Paraka's tribesmen sometimes went to help to complete the work. The building of aid posts, schools, mission station, airstrips and bridges was also needed. The patrol officers engaged the bosbois to interview and recruit people to do all the work. Because they respected the patrol officers and feared the bosbois the tribesmen worked hard at their job.

When they were required to build a house for the white men to sleep or for any public use, the members of the community would quickly respond and build it. There was some form of division of labour whereby some brought kunai grass while the others brought blinds for the walls and the timbers for the post or rafters and in a day a house was completed. There was co-operation between the people of different clans and tribes in the activities that were taking place.

Paraka was still young in those times and was unable to help the people of his tribe in building houses, bridges and roads but fetched water and brought food for them. Building of roads was a wearisome experience and at the same time it was very enjoyable from what Paraka saw as a youngster. Every morning at around five o'clock his uncle Koembo, the bosboi, would call for all the tribesmen and women to wake up and get ready to build roads. Paraka could still remember, the men were ready outside their houses hours before bosboi Koembo called. That happened because traditionally men were encouraged to stay out of their houses in the early hours of the mornings to avoid being attacked by the rival tribes. When everyone was awake they all went down to the site where the new road was to be built and started working.

The work of building roads was assigned equally among different tribes in Baiyer. The bosbois ensured that each part assigned to a tribe was expected to be done and completed. Nii did not go to work and stayed at home one day thinking that Koembo would be biased and have mercy on him. Instead Koembo was searching for Nii among other people who already turned up for work. He realised that Nii and Paraka did not go to work so when he came home and saw them at home he hit his brother very hard with his cane stick. Afraid that his uncle would hit him also Paraka climbed up a tree close by. Koembo stripped Nii naked and took him to the place where the others were working. Paraka climbed down the tree to follow them. Koembo teased Nii by telling all the men to look at the naked man. He hit him again with his cane in front of everyone. Koembo warned all the men there that if he could hit his own brother that hard then others had to expect the worst if they disobeyed like Nii.

When the rest of the men from Paraka's tribe heard that Koembo had warned them, they whispered quietly to each other saying, 'that is true, he is a strict man'. Everyone from the tribe feared Koembo and never missed a day's work. Not only did Paraka's tribesmen fear him but all the other men, women and children of the Baiyer and the Lumusa area feared him. Whenever Koembo went for a visit to a particular village, people walking along the track would hide in order to avoid seeing him. After he had passed they came out of their hiding places to continue their journey. Others killed pigs and roasted them for him when they heard that he was paying a visit to their village.

The trees from the edge of the big rain forest between Madang and Western Highlands were chopped down and cut to size to build the bridges. The men pulled the logs towards the bank of the Baiyer River then managed to deliver them to the site where a bridge was to be built. The logs were meters wide and about sixty to one hundred meters in length requiring the entire tribe or two to pull such a log.

The experience was new to the people and even though it was an expensive and tiring exercise, everyone loved the task. The men tied a rope or two on to each of the logs and pulled it one at a time. As they were putting all their strength together to pull the log, they sang traditional songs that signified that they enjoyed pulling the logs. The danger in that particular work was that the logs sometimes ran over some men when they came at very high speeds. They died on the spot. The bridges would be built as soon as the logs reached the riverbank. The first vehicles to run on the roads and bridges were those owned by the patrol officers, and those trucks were called Mini Mork (Mini Moke) or Holden.

While the patrol officers were working to bring people from different tribes together to work in groups the missionaries arrived. They were very friendly and kind to the people preaching to them that they should not hate each other but to love one another. Peace was established among the tribes along the Baiyer valley. The Australian

Baptist missionaries succeeded in stopping the tribal fights that Paraka's tribe had endured for years. Initially it was thought that what the white men said was fairy tales but as time passed they came to accept that what the missionaries said was true. The whole tribe from Baiyer trusted them and followed their preaching.

The Christian religion of the white missionaries did not feel foreign to Lengame. She already firmly believed that it was God the father who was listening to her and had worked a miracle for her through giving her a son, Paraka. Today she is very old and has witnessed the lives of her great-great grandchildren. She cannot read but can memorise bible verses and often asks her literate sons and grandchildren to read bible stories to her. She does not miss Sunday church services and often talks about the love of Jesus Christ.

One of her unique features is her application of the word Love. She loves everyone and hates none regardless of whether they are her relatives or not. She has the heart for everyone. She speaks of God and the love of Jesus Christ every time I visit her.

"Love your enemies, as you love your brothers and sisters, you must feed them when they are hungry, and you must shelter them when they need it."

Those are the words she taught me from an early age.

Apart from spreading the gospel, the Baptist missionaries established a small aid post later expanded to become a hospital, which is known today as the Tinsley Hospital along with a school of nursing. It was where I was born in 1979.

Paraka's men also helped to build an airstrip that is used today by the Missionaries Aviation Fellowship (MAF), a mission owned aircraft. As Paraka was growing up he thought all those things that they helped to complete were for the good of the white men. He eventually realised that they were established for the good of the whole Baiyer population.

CHAPTER 7

ENROLLED AT MISSION SCHOOL

In 1956 Paraka and his family still lived at Maralama. When he heard the story of a white woman who visited Jukuna, a village on the mountain several kilometres away from his home every Sunday for church services his interest was piqued.

One Sunday, he sat with the other boys and girls surrounding Miss Marsden who produced an organ and began playing melodious music with her fingers. Paraka became a regular at Sunday school to see and hear more of the organ and music.

He was 17 years old.

Paraka had very big sores on his stomach that took ages to heal up. However, the white lady cleaned those sores and put some white stuff on them. Over the next few days he was amazed to notice that the sores had gradually started to heal.

As they gathered around her as usual on a Sunday during their Sunday school class, she said something in English, translated to them by a local translator. There was going to be something that was known as school. They did not know what school was but they were eager to go and discover this new thing. So far, they had seen miraculous things such as the healing of sores and producing harmonious music from the organ so they were prompted to go to see more.

Marsden said that school was going to be held at Kumbareta the following week and she wanted them to be there very early in the morning on that day.

Paraka went home and told his parents about it and asked them if he could go but they refused. They thought he would feel hungry while at school and were afraid that this would lead him to eat poisoned food offered by their enemies. The other reason was that their parents thought their enemies would shoot him with a bow and arrow while walking to or from school. His colleagues, Kiap and Raima also got the same response from their parents. No matter how many times they had pleaded with their parents to let them go to Sunday school both parents refused.

Their parents were accustomed to their own culture and traditions and they were not convinced of the strange concept that the white men had introduced. They wanted their children to remain in the village and take part in the ceremonies such as making moka and grow to take part in their tribal warfare. Their parents did not want any of them to be indoctrinated with the white man's tradition that they thought was useless or not worth learning. They passionately wanted to maintain their own customs and traditions.

Paraka and his friends disagreed with their parents. They were ambitious to discover more of those strange things so Paraka decided to find a way to get around the parents' instructions to stay away. He gathered a few of the boys of his age group namely, Raima, Kiap and Lasi and told them that they were going to go to school tomorrow without letting their parents know. They all agreed as each did not want to miss out on the interesting things that the white people had and did. That afternoon they took off to another place to stay overnight at a small hut that was built near the Laka creek without any food, making sure that they went downhill to spend the night

By evening they were very hungry. There was a garden within walking distance but it was not of their families. However, it belonged to a family within their own tribe so they quietly walked into the garden without being noticed and got some aibika, banana and corn for the night. Unfortunately, this was the only source of food for the night that they roasted and ate for dinner but they were still very hungry. The hut was so cold although they made a very big fire to keep themselves warm through the night. There was nowhere else for them to go but to sleep there till day break. The chilled night made them restless and their sleep was unwelcoming but they tried their best to sleep.

At dawn the wakeful songs of birds awoke them up from their undisturbed but uncomfortable sleep. Upon waking up they rushed down to the river and took a very cold bath each. There was no soap so they did not get rid of their dirt but just dived into the creek and climbed out shivering.

By then it was already broad daylight so they wanted to arrive at Kumbareta very early in the morning as the white lady had instructed them to do. They ran as fast as they could to warm up their numb bodies and to be there on time. They were not only on time, but the first before the rest of the students turned up for the lesson.

Their teacher was a white man accompanied by a native translator. On the first day at school, the white man explained what school was with the help of some drawings on the blackboard. For example, he drew a picture of a banana tree on the blackboard and asked the boys to name it in their Kyaka language. They answered that it was called Kyaeya. He also drew a different picture of a pig like animal in which they gave the language name for it as mena. Though the communication with the white man was not direct, what he said was translated to them only by the native. They were not taught other new things apart from the pictures and their names spoken in their own language. The introductory lessons were indeed more helpful to the white man himself using the boys as a means through which the white man could learn the boys' language.

After the first day of school they went back to the hut where they had stayed last night. They felt reluctant to go home because they were afraid of their parents' beatings. Therefore, they had to force themselves to survive in that hut in spite of hunger and cold. They did not want to live on aibika and corn alone so Paraka displayed his initiative and took on the role of their leader.

Two kilometres west from where they stayed was Lengame's place or garden. Paraka decided to go there to collect some food for all of them. He dug enough sweet potatoes to last them for the night and returned to the hut. Meanwhile the other boys collected firewood. They cooked enough sweet potatoes for their dinner with some left over for the next day. Unlike the previous morning, they woke up a little bit later at around 6.30 am to get ready for school. They knew now that school was not going to start as early as they thought. They had their bath and sat next to the fire to get themselves dried and warm. They walked to school arriving there just on time.

As they waited for the school bell to ring, a man by the name of Kulg, a translator and relative of Paraka, arrived. Grabbing the surprised Paraka by the neck, Kulg began hitting and belting the would-be student. Kulg blamed Paraka for the theft of his new aluminium cooking pot which he had gotten from the white man. In fact Paraka did not steal it but because it went missing Kulg claimed that Paraka had stolen it on their first day at school

As the bell rang for class to commence they all went into the classroom and sat down. Paraka was howling with every eye staring at him; even his comrades. He could not concentrate on the lesson and felt deeply hurt. As he sat there he questioned himself, "why did I come to school and get beaten up like this?" He thought school was a good thing but such circumstances and problems made him disillusioned and he gave up hope of going to school again.

After school ended that day Lasi, Kiap, Raima and Paraka decided that they would go back to Maralama. They had encountered enough problems with food, the sleepless chilled nights, followed by Paraka being beaten. So they strolled uphill to their village just a little fearful of what they might encounter.

When questioned by his parents as to where he had been for two nights Paraka refused to tell them his story. His father sternly

ENROLLED AT MISSION SCHOOL

promised a beating if he kept going to school but Paraka knew deep in his heart he would go again even though there might be consequences.

The following morning Lasi, Kiap, Raima and Paraka went and took a bath each and sneaked off to school. It took them only an hour to walk the distance so they arrived just on time. As usual the bell rang, they all went in and waited quietly for the white man to teach them. They learnt basically the same things as the other days. Eventually they learned so many new things including the alphabetical letters and some new words, which they were purposely taught in order that the white man understood the language. Hence, this pattern of teaching went on for about three to four months. After the first few days that they went to school, the parents tried every possible way to stop them from going. When they finally realised that the boys were genuinely interested in learning, they woke them up very early in the mornings to cook their breakfast and lunch and help them get ready for school. They ate some kaukau in the mornings and took the rest for lunch. To overcome their fear that enemies would offer their children food, the mothers made sure that they took enough food to feed the boys' hunger. To overcome their fear that enemies would poison their food if left outside before going in for class, the boys hid their lunches a distance away from the school so that nobody would notice their actions.

Gradually teacher and student came to understand each other better. The need for translations began to diminish. One day during class, their teacher told his students that there would be rewards to those who answered his questions correctly. Paraka wanted to win the clothes and soap prizes so he usually put his hands up first to call out the answers. Sometimes he was right but other times wrong. When he took those things home and showed them to his parents, they were very impressed. All negative comments and frightening remarks about the white men's concepts, including the introduction of new things such as school, started to diminish. When school ended for the year all the boys were on holidays, another new concept to embrace. After the break they went back to school in the new-year to study grade 2.

It was 1957. Paraka would turn 18 years old.

He did not finish the school year. His parents, particularly his father and his Uncle Koembo had found a wife for him. A lady from the UkuniOimbo tribe, twice as old as Paraka age, was being pre-arranged as his wife. Since Paraka was still a teenager, he was frightened of the idea of marriage. This young man with shattered dreams of unfulfilled hopes wondered why he had to leave school while his friends Kiap, Lasi and Raima were still going. Even though Paraka did not like his chosen bride, he was forced to accept the arrangement. Unlike this twenty first century, where new partners engage in marriage through love according to their own choices and interest, this era for Paraka was a quite different story.

This stubborn student clung to his belief he should attend school as he yearned to learn new things. Back in the school room, the teacher embarrassed him in front of everyone by saying, 'you are married now, so you must never come back to school. Only single people can attend, not married people." He was shocked and embarrassed at the same time by such a statement. Mixing his new foreign language and his native Kyaka he tried to explain to the teacher that the lady was not his wife. She was as his father's third wife. The teacher was not convinced and insisted that he should leave the school. Paraka felt that it was the end of his world. He wept bitterly. Reluctantly he left the schoolyard and returned home. Paraka felt defeated because no one defended him to allow him stay in school, everyone wanted him to leave school. He grew angrier with his parents and relatives for getting a wife for him, a lady called Simbu, who remains the first of his five wives today.

Three days after leaving school, Paraka ran away to work on a farm, away from his embarrassment that he was to stay at home and take Simbu as his wife.

In his despair he found a beacon of light when he recalled that his Uncle Koembo had promised him that he would take over Koembo's luluai position when he retired. He believed Koembo because he was a luluai and a very prominent person that time so he thought Koemba would not lie to him. He had something to look forward to but was determined to learn the ways of the white men.

CHAPTER 8

WORKED WITH THE AUSTRALIAN FARMERS

There was a big farm run by Australians a few kilometers away from the school and Paraka headed there to learn more about the white men. In the morning he stood in the line with all the other farmers hoping to be picked by the Australian farmer, George Bill. He chose all the other laborers but when he came to Paraka he did not pick him thinking he was too young. If only he had read Paraka's intentions and desires on how enthusiastically he wanted to work there, that he wanted to go to work and live on the farm to avoid all the disappointment and defeats that he had received earlier.

Paraka did not anticipate that such a thing would happen to him so as soon as he realised that he was not going to be picked, he felt very upset. Not wanting to return to his home, not wanted at the farm, this disconsolate man went to Kaleta, the home of the neighbouring Sipani tribe. He stayed the night with Yaga Pana, a pastor of the Australian Baptist church. Even though this pastor was not a relative Paraka knew very well that he was going to be safe because Yaga Pana was not from the enemy tribe and was a servant of God. As Paraka rested during the night, his initiative bloomed. He was convinced he could get the white man to accept him as a worker at the farm.

He woke up very early in the morning and dressed in Yaga Pana's traditional costumes. He had no beard but in order to gain one, he rubbed charcoal on his face. He tied an oversized bark belt around his waist which was loose and almost fell but made sure that it was held up against his waist. On his front he wore a malo which was woven from bush twines. He covered his buttocks with tanget leaves. He ran to the farm after he got dressed and stood in the line with the other laborers to be picked and assigned to various jobs by George Bill. He stood in suspense as to whether or not the white man would recognise him for the second time. Fortunately, George Bill thought Paraka was one of those older men so he assigned him to a job with the other labourers. It was the happiest moment of his life because he wanted so much to work on the farm and he was prepared to work very hard.

When he came to supervise on the second day, George Bill was amazed to see Paraka working with the other labourers. Paraka saw the disbelief on George's face and expected him to ask him to leave the farm instantly. However, he never did. Instead he appointed Paraka to take charge at cleaning the flower gardens around the farm. He worked very hard and the boss was pleased with him so he did not appoint another person.

George Bill and Paraka became very good friends. The white man trusted him and let him do as much work as he wanted to do during the day without supervision. However, Paraka thought it was unfair on the other labourers so he did as much work as they did. When he finished doing his own labouring he approached Nukunts, the cook, and offered to help in the kitchen washing the dishes. All the farm laborers worked very hard for little pay. They were given axes, clothes and mirrors, but those items were very special to them back then as they learned to appreciate how much faster they could chop down a tree with the axe faster than their fathers' times when it would take almost a month to cut down a huge tree with the stone axe.

Every afternoon after work, worn out from hard labour, the labourers took a bath in the nearby creek then rested in their small huts built on the farm. Often some of the men were interested in attending a Tanim het, a traditional form of courtship where young people get together in a house and sing songs while a few young men and women go through the courtship ritual.

Paraka thought he was too young to take part in activities in which women were involved but he went there for the first time to see what it was that attracted every man from the farm. As he sat with the others as a spectator, he became very interested and finally decided to try it.

Paraka had been forced to marry prior to his joining the farm but he never consummated the responsibilities of a husband with his wife. To this effect, he still looked very young and innocent. So many young ladies who were there asked him to court them in the tanim het but he refused. It was his first time and he was quite nervous that he would do the wrong thing altogether. He finally submitted and agreed to court a young lady called Pen from the Kimbin tribe of Baiyer. Pen was an experienced person whereas Paraka was not but she did not tell him how to start or what to do. They sat there totally confused while the other partners proceeded with the process of courting.

When others had finished courting for the first round of songs, Paraka's friends realised that he had not started yet so they began teasing him, then showed him how to do it. A couple of head turns first by the nervous young man was followed by Pen making another couple of heads turns. The next step was one in which Pen and Paraka touched each other's faces, especially their noses and then nodded their heads together. However, before they got it right Paraka made a couple of head turns very quickly, then Pen did likewise. Instead of them bringing their faces together at the same time so that their noses touched, Paraka leaned forward and pulled her nose towards him with his fingers in a very rough manner. He could have hurt her but she did not complain.

The other men who had watched him all laughed and started teasing him. Paraka was fed up and embarrassed so he left the place very quietly and went back to the farm unnoticed. From then on he never went back because he did not want to see the lady again. Tanim het was also held in a lot of other places so he went to those and learnt a lot about the process. He became a champion at the required tasks and met so many young ladies who became his girlfriends. One of those was Pokel from the UkuniKapelgambo tribe. Pokel asked Paraka to go to Kaleta so that they could court in the Tanim het. She said several men had asked her to go there so that they could court with her but she was particularly interested in courting with Paraka.

In the afternoons after work Paraka and his mates all made sure that they had enough to eat for the night especially when they were to go out courting. One day, Paraka finished work in the afternoon earlier than usual and prepared to go to Kaleta as Pokel had asked him to do the other night. He quickly cooked some sweet potatoes or kaukau, went down to the creek and took a bath. After he came up from the creek, he quickly ate his evening meal. He did not wait for the others but started walking at dusk but soon the others came and caught up with him.

On his arrival Paraka was dismayed to notice that others who had arrived earlier had already started, including Pokel. She was courting with some other men which made Paraka upset because he had purposely gone there at her invitation. Paraka knew he had to do something to convince Pokel to leave those she was courting with and to join him. At last he went outside and chanted a song in the Melpa language to convince her to change her mind and to indicate to her that he was upset by what she was doing. This song is sung by a male party on special occasions, such as the courtship or other ceremonial events, to indicate to the others that they are not happy with the way they have been treated.

"Eroidenwai a, Baiyermolgopolgadopkant

mel a Kaletaku o de pengbonemen o we

EroIdenwai a wampelpamulkonaprennuman

Wang dokonnan o eroIdenwai a" (2x)

As soon as Pokel heard the song she felt very upset. She knew that it was Paraka whom she had asked to court her. She left all the men whom she was courting with and ran into the bedroom and wept. That made the men very angry. They rushed outside to fight Paraka because they knew that he was the one who made her leave them and go. Paraka and the men fought seriously for some time until others stepped in and stopped the fighting. After the incident, and before Paraka departed, Pokel asked him to go to Dekenpana, a place of the Ukunilineag, in a few days so that they could make up for the opportunity that they had missed.

Several days later, Paraka walked excitedly to Dekenpana accompanied with a few of his labourer friends. Before they went to the house of Tanim het, they visited at his patrimonial cousin's house at BanermTraliya, the first daughter of Paraka's uncle Koembo, was close to Paraka. It was customary practice that participants of the Tanim het courtship were to stay at the common house during the night.

After dinner the Tanim het session commenced. Even though, there were a lot of young girls waiting and ready to participate in the courtship ritual, Paraka spent the evening occupied with Pokel alone because he had purposely gone there at her invitation. He kept his attention on Pokel too scared that she would harm him if he did not.

Around 4am as the first light of dawn appeared on the horizon Pokel said to Paraka, "give me your ears."

Surprised at what she was going to say, he moved his ears closer. She whispered "can you go outside and meet me at a site which is cleared to make a new garden within the next 20 minutes. I will wait for you there."

"Ok." Paraka replied almost instantly. "I will do as you ask."

Paraka did not understand why she wanted him to go but he was eager to find out why. He kept it to himself not telling anyone, believing that no one knew or saw what was going on between them. An elderly man from Paraka's village approached him curious to know what he had been told when Pokel whispered to his ears. Paraka told the man what he was told. The old man interpreted the request as the possibility that either she was going to kill him or had arranged for someone else to do the job. Paraka did not hesitate. He ran as fast as he could back to the farm.

The daily grind of work on the farm rarely varied until the day two cooks fought.

One was Trakalowa, Paraka's tribesman and the other Nukunts from the Kilimbi clan of the Kumdi lineage, cook for the labourers. Trakalowa was a one-eyed man who had lost one of his eyes when attacked by a wild pig. He was the cook for their new boss Danny Leah, while George Bill was on leave. Trakalowa was a fearsome giant while Nukunts was dwarf size in comparison. Nukunts was wounded badly by Trakalowa. When all Kumdi men on the farm saw how seriously Nukunts was wounded badly by Trakalowa, they mobbed up and took revenge on the boss's cook.

The fight had started when Trakalowa went straight into the mess without asking Nukunts politely if he could eat something from the mess. Nukunt's anger flared at the rudeness of Trakalowa, not standing in the queue with the others who were also very hungry. To cool his anger Nukunts scolded Trakalowa in front of everyone. Trakalowa threw his fists in reply at Nukunts.

Paraka was right there with the others and watched the fight but did not bother to interfere until Nukunts was badly wounded. When the Kumdi took revenge on Trakalowa, Paraka was very sorry to see Trakalowa so seriously wounded but felt impotent due to his youth to attack older men. He squatted near his tribal relation and recommended that they wait until their new boss, Danny returned from Mount Hagen town.

Paraka hid behind bushes a few kilometres away from the farm shed, waiting for the boss's return. As soon as he saw dust rising from the road some distance away, he went out to the road, signalled the driver to stop. Paraka reported everything that had happened between the two men but in his bias towards Trakalowa, he said that Nukunts was only punched once. He cried so loudly that his tribesmen thought he was indeed badly wounded. This statement was indeed false. In fact, Nukunts was badly bitten several times by Trakalowa.

Paraka continued with his tale, telling Danny that it was Trakalowa who was almost killed by the Kumdi men just because Nukunts cried. Danny was furious. Trakalowa was his cook so he told Paraka to hop on to the car so that they could drive to the farm and solve the problem. Paraka was hesitant to go because he did not want it to be obvious that he had reported the incident to Danny. Therefore, he said that he wanted to walk to the farm. Mr. Leahy understood and drove off.

As soon as Danny got out of his car, he went straight to Nukunts and grabbed his arms, lifted him right up and then dropped him to the ground. As Nukunts fell, Danny lifted his knees up and hit Nukunts so hard that it broke his jaw. Through the night, Nukunts was taken to Kumbareta aid post.

Retaliation was the only thing on the minds of Nukunts' tribesmen. All night they hunted for the Kyakini but could not find a single one as all had escaped. Only Paraka remained. Fearful of retribution he headed for an empty hut where food was normally cooked. As the hours passed he started to believe he would be saved from a brutal beating. That changed when he heard some men talking outside the hut deciding to check on whether or not someone was hiding in the hut. Paraka shivered with fear as he silently prayed for the men to go away.

Before they went away Paraka heard one of them say to the others in Melpa language that all the Kyakini men were gone and the door was locked. He suggested that they go down to the creek to check in case they would find someone there. This is exactly what Paraka heard:

> *"Manga kumba petem kant o, wubo pong kant o*
>
> *mereng nu wungela ping ken kanamen."*

And they all went down to the creek. That moment was one of the happiest of Paraka's life because he had almost been discovered and wounded but had fortunately survived. He was sure that no one was outside so he opened the door very quietly, making sure that it did not make any noise and went outside. The next safest place that Paraka thought of was Danny's place so he headed away from his hiding place very quietly. Danny had a fierce dog that barked loudly when sensing Paraka's approach.

"Who's outside?" yelled Danny.

"All the Kyakini men have run away through fear of being attacked by the Kumdi. I am the only one here on the farm. Could I stay with you tonight?" yelled Paraka.

Danny kindly did. In the morning both tribes lined up for roll call. The Kumdi men pretended that nothing had happened during the night and that Danny was unaware of the fight.

Shock set in when they heard Danny's words.

"During the night all of you went around hunting for men and now you are pretending as if nothing had happened, you bloody kanakas." After he scolded them, he fired all of them from work so they went home weeping bitterly because working with the white men was something very special to them and they felt very proud. After losing their jobs on the farm the Kumdi men sang a song that they were not happy with someone for reporting to Danny about the incident which took place in the night. The song they sang was:

"Rake linga kepal, a Rake linga kepal a, na

wur el ip tip o lgo, lgo

paeii o we e wai o pa eii o

Danny kangem a komon ralgnana

Jandapko pent o, lgo, lgo

Pa eii o we e wai o pa eii o we e."

After the Kumdi men had left the farm, peace and quiet reigned. One day an elderly man from Kumdi came to ask for work on the farm. Danny felt sorry for him so he gave him a job. By then Paraka had been appointed a supervisor to take on work that Danny no longer wished to do.

In his role as supervisor he made sure that his tribesmen did not do the most difficult jobs. He told them go to the creek to catch fish and hunt bandicoot but when they saw Danny coming to supervise, they were to come up from the creek and pretend to be working very hard. His tribesmen noted the good things Paraka did for them and often talked together about his being a good leader to take the place of his father and uncle in the future.

One day Danny killed a cow for them in appreciation of the hard work that they did on the farm. The elderly man from Kumdi and Paraka were told to prepare the mumu while the rest of the men went to work as usual. The two of them prepared, operated, and roasted the cow in the pit. After they made the mumu, they sat around waiting for it to cook. The old man cooked a piece of meat that he cut out from the cow separately. Paraka was scared and did not want to be part of the theft because if they were caught stealing, they would be fired from the farm.

The man cut a piece from the cooked bit of meat and passed it to Paraka who refused to eat. He strongly suspected that the meat was poisoned. The old man insisted that he eat the meat so they would not be caught. They were still arguing over the small meat when all the labourers returned from work. Paraka did not want them to know about the situation so hid the meat without anyone else noticing. The hungry men ate and enjoyed the prepared cow departing to their respective house or farm huts. Paraka remained convinced that the meat was poisoned. He took it with him to his hut, hung the meat in between the rafters of the hut to examine what would happen during the night or the next day, if in fact it was poisoned.

Paraka woke up and looked to see what was happening on the spot where he hid the meat. To his surprise, he saw light twinkling and grease dripping down from the spot. He grew frightened of the strange thing that had happened to the meat so he pulled it down, took it outside and threw it away. A drip of grease from the meat fell on his thumb and as it was poisoned, a very big and painful sore grew on his skin. He had to stop working on the farm and went home because he could not bear the pain from the poisoned sore any longer. He had been away three years.

His parents, his wife and all of his relatives were very happy to have him home again. Paraka visited the Kumbareta aid post often in order to heal his sore. The nurse gave him some tablets to take every time he went there and gradually the sore started to heal up. He took so many tablets of the same kind that he grew familiar with the names of each such as disprin and aspirin. One day at the aid post he told the nurse, a white man, which tablets he was supposed to give him. Surprised, the nurse asked Paraka how he got to know the names of each of the tablets. Had been to school to learn such names. Paraka's reply was even more surprising.

"I haven't been to school and nobody taught me. I just knew it somehow."

The white man was very impressed and invited Paraka to help him with work at the aid post. His job was to call the names of the patients so that the white man did not have to do everything at the same time. Paraka rejoiced in his new found responsibilities as he knew this was another opportunity to work with a white man again.

One day as Paraka was working he saw his cousin, Kungu Papa fighting with Laliwa because Laliwa was having an affair for a long time with Kungu's wife. Paraka was so furious with Laliwa for doing such a thing to this cousin, Kungu, he hit Laliwa hard on the neck causing blood to flow. When his boss heard of Paraka's involvement in the fight, he sacked him from working at the aid post.

CHAPTER 9

PARENTS DIVORCED

In 1959 Nii divorced his wife, Lengame as he feared she might poison him or others of his tribe. Lengame was of the Senapunyi tribe, members of which were suspected of poisoning one of Nii's tribesmen, Otenga. Fear and suspicion were daily companions causing the end of a once strong marriage.

The Nii family had moved from their old home at Maralama and settled at Ambetau, a place in the Baiyer valley at the foot of the mountain. Paraka brought Simbu, his wife of one year to join his younger brothers, Peng, Puri, Moka and Nentepa to stay with their mother Lengame at the home of their Uncle Gaiyer of the Senapun tribe.

Nii lived with his other wife Dawe and her children Napil, Tiptip, Kilt and Ketepa.

At this same time, the new concept of ward council was introduced by the then Australian Colonial Administrators. Since there were no men who could match Paraka in terms of how he could change everything through the power of his speech even at an early age, he was undisputedly elected as the councillor of the *Kyakini* tribe in 1964. He was 25 years old and still living with his Uncle Gaiyer.

After five years living with his uncle, Paraka realised that there was not enough land for him and his younger brothers to stay permanently. However, at his father's place there was so much uncultivated land waiting to be claimed. Paraka also recognised that anybody who built a house and made a garden for the first time on a piece of land, claimed ownership over that land. He believed it was likely that a hard working person could possibly build many houses, make many vegetable gardens and as a result be able to acquire many lands.

Paraka was made a leader and built a home next to the newly built road linking Baiyer River and Mount Hagen. He was certain that living next to the road would bring them good fortune. His mother, the four brothers plus two born while living with their uncle plus his wife Simbu were invited to live in the house.

Slowly gardens sprung up around the house while a very small trading store was built mainly of kunai grass and branches from the treetops and bushes around Marlama and Kontopeg. All the brothers worked on the project and in a short time goods were being sold.

Peace was shattered when men from Lengame's tribe built a couple of houses around Paraka's and claimed ownership over that same land. Paraka insisted that he had settled there first and that they should vacate the land and leave in order to avoid problems. They refused. Finally the dispute was taken to court.

In those days, Patrol Officers heard the claims in the local courts in the Baiyer District. Judgments were made according to the nature of the cause. In few cases there was danger that favouritism and nepotism was likely to be practised by the Patrol Officers.

While waiting for his case to be heard, Paraka returned work on the farm where George Bill was manager. When some of the men suing him arrived to inform him that the court case was to be heard that day, Paraka was indeed surprised.

He looked for George Bill to seek permission to leave the property but could not find him so together the men headed down the dusty road.

As a car approached Paraka strained his eyes to figure out whose vehicle it was and recognised it was George Bill's car carrying his wife and children home from school. The car stopped at Paraka's signal. He explained his need to go to court and asked her to explain to her husband. She promised him she would and drove away with her children.

Twenty minutes later another car threw up dust. This time it was George Bill.

The car stopped in front of them and George told Paraka to get into his car. While Bill was driving Paraka explained that the case was over land dispute. After listening carefully to his story, George promised him that he would convince the Patrol officer to make the decision in Paraka's favour.

The moment he saw George Bill coming out of the office he knew that he had finished talking with the Patrol officer. Later all the men were called into the office of the Patrol officer and the hearing of the case commenced. The Patrol Officer, an Australian, had asked each of them to give their side of the story on why and how they were claiming ownership of the land. Paraka's opponents gave their side of the story and he presented his after them. The Patrol officer pretended he was disseminating justice in front of everyone even though he had reached his decision earlier in favour of Paraka. After having heard all their stories the Officer declared Paraka as the rightful owner of the land. The opponents were told to move which they did without any trouble.

When he was 28 years old, Paraka finished the work on the farm and moved home to stay with the rest of his family members. Not long after that, his Uncle Koembo asked him to go live with him on his land. Paraka agreed leaving the brothers, his mother and wife behind at the home in Kuipbout.

Paraka worked hard building gardens and planting coffee trees. His uncle asked him to find some money somewhere so that they could buy cattle for Paraka to look after. Excited with these new and helpful ideas, he went and asked his maternal uncles to give him some money. He returned to Koembo's house with AUD$300. They bought ten head of cattle with that money and some of their own. In those times a cow cost fifty dollars, a bull thirty dollars.

Koembo was very pleased with Paraka's hard work so one day he called him into his house at midday when everyone else was still working in the garden. They sat on the floor facing each other. The uncle started the conversation.

"You and your brothers are like orphans, without a father so you all have to be self-reliant." He continued "A lazy man is unable to live on his own so he becomes dependent on others however, a hard working person always has enough to eat."

Paraka nodded agreeably already aware of those things and putting them into practice. While he was advising him Koembo expressed his disappointment to see Nii forgetting Paraka and his brothers. Paraka sat quietly while he listened to the words that lifted his spirits. Koembo was granting him a large area of land for Paraka's cattle.

"Make a fence using posts and barbed wires" his uncle said and within a few weeks the fence was finished. The cattle were transferred across to the new yard. After some time Paraka owned more than a hundred cows with the numbers increasing regularly. Gradually the cows were sold for payment of bride prices, compensation payment and other expenses. While he was selling the cattle, he also made sure that his store was fully stocked. As there was little competition, Paraka made good money.

During this time in history George Bill and the Patrol Officer owned the only vehicles that travelled along the road at Mt Hagen and Baiyer. When men from the Troepo tribe asked Koembo and Paraka to help contribute money to buy a vehicle, Paraka suggested to Koembo that they also buy one for themselves. Paraka asked his uncle Gaiyer again to loan him money, which he did.

PARENTS DIVORCED

Early the next morning both men set out walking to Mount Hagen town. Upon arriving at Olgulpeng, a place of a Lutheran Mission few kilometres north of Mt Hagen, it was dark so they slept in a makeshift hut. Early the next morning, they continued to Mt Hagen arriving at the car sales yard.

The white man who was in charge of the sale of vehicles that they wanted to buy told them that the vehicle had not arrived from Lae so he asked them to come back the next day. Koembo and Paraka stayed in town with a friend of Koembo who was a white man.

The next day they bought a Toyota Stout at a cost of A$2,500.

Neither of the two men knew how to drive a car. Only white men could do that so Paraka was determined to earn the respect and admiration of his people. As with many times during his life, help appeared when he needed it. Koembo's friend, a white man, taught Paraka the fundamentals of driving. After a couple of days practice, he drove to his home. Only white men drove cars so when his people saw him at the wheel in control of the car, they began to treat him as they did a white man.

He used the vehicle to transport cattle and brought new store goods from Mount Hagen. The concept of charging people to use the vehicle for transport was not in existence but in due time this changed and income from transporting people increased. Paraka was the first councillor to own a vehicle within the Baiyer district and always drove to his council meetings. People liked him and his fame spread throughout the Baiyer, Mul and Lumusa areas.

By the time he was 30 years old at the end of 1969, he had married five wives.

His life was full of responsibility. He attended council meetings, managed his small trading store, looked after his cattle and cared for his mother, his wives and younger brothers.

Puri, number two son, was born in 1944 at Marlama in Kyakinyi tribe of Baiyer area. He married four wives and I am the first born by his fourth wife. As a young man my father was aggressive and fearless. Other youths of his age jumped at his commands.

In 1952 he was enrolled at Endarmarn elementary school, a newly established institution by the Australian Baptist Missionary but relinquished studies and later went to Hagen Tea School for his studies, leaving school at third grade.

In 1965, he became a driver with the West Highlands Province government. Five years later he left driving and went to Baiyer where he became a cowboy in the newly established Baiyer Live Stock Development Corporation. After ten years he left this work and went back to his tribe in 1975.

Since my father was well acquainted with native laws and customs, he was appointed the local village court magistrate for Kuipboat village and the overall chairman of the Baiyer area the following year at the age of 32. He is currently the Chairman of all Magistrates in Baiyer and the Magistrate of Kuipboat area.

Paraka's third brother, Peng, enrolled at the Bomana Police College in the National Capital District training as a Cadet Officer. He graduated as a sub-Inspector and later changed his name to Bill who is now deceased.

Moka and Nentepa, fourth and fifth born respectively, helped Paraka at the store and with his cattle.

The sixth child was called John. When he enrolled in school he thought his family name was Paraka as his father Nii had not been in his life. One morning after John had gone to school without eating any breakfast his mother stood outside the classroom. The white female teacher went out and asked his mother whom she was waiting to visit. Lengame told the teacher that she was waiting for a grade one student by the name of John Nii. The teacher told her that there was nobody by that name in class but Lengame insisted that there was one and it was her son.

The teacher went inside and asked a number of boys whose names were John, if they had Nii as their surname. None responded. The white lady went outside and told Lengame that John Nii was not in her class. Lengame still insisted that her son was in the class. At last the teacher asked Lengame to stand at the door and check if her son was in her class. Lengame did, pointing to her son. She explained that Paraka was his elder brother so John changed his surname to Nii on the roll.

The baby of the family at that time was the seventh born, Yapo.

Paraka fenced various areas around the small cattle farm and made some gardens for the five wives. His father, Nii, and his step-brothers grew jealous believing Paraka was trying to occupy all the land through the pretext of making gardens. They sent messages to him through various people advising him not to continue making gardens but he did not listen to them.

Frustrated, his step-brothers retaliated by cutting the barb wire fence of the cattle farm with pliers. As a result the cattle escaped and accessed other people's gardens destroying all their food crops.

The owners of the gardens blamed Paraka time after time for not fixing the fence. Despite their blame, Paraka was not willing to fix the fence because he knew that the step-brothers and father would cut the wires again. Many of the cattle went over to the former Baiyer River Livestock Development Corporation cattle farm where Paraka found it hard to identify which of them were his. The cattle remaining on the farm were sold and Paraka sold the land equally shared among the brothers, except Bill who was in the police force.

The step-brothers and Nii also wanted a share of the land but Paraka refused their repeated requests which led to a dispute. The step-brothers and Nii uprooted all the food crops that grew in their new gardens. Disgruntled and angry, Paraka's brothers did likewise to the others' gardens. Paraka pleaded with his brothers not to seek revenge but they were angry with their father for mistreating them and divorcing their mother. The rivalry went on for more than a year and no form of compromise could be reached. Prison cells awaited many of them.

In 1979, Nentepa made a garden on a piece of land that was formally their mother's garden. Their step-brothers led by their father went over to where Nentepa was working and demanded that he should stop working. Nentepa refused, a quarrel broke out which resulted in a fist fight. Nentepa knew that they were many fighting against him alone so he fought only for a short while then he ran away.

Paraka and his other brothers saw Nentepa running to them exhausted, scratches all over his body. When he told his brothers what had happened, they grabbed their bows and arrows and sought revenge. Some of the houses on either side were burnt to ashes, gardens were destroyed and many were wounded. Only Puri and Yapo were not involved.

The following day the police came and arrested every one of them involved in the fight, including those who were not part of the family but had participated, and sent them to prison. Puri did not go to prison because he did not fight. He stayed at home and looked after their mother, Paraka's wives and the children and those of the other brothers.

Those who went to prison spent the first night in the cell in Hagen, which was the most terrible place on this whole earth. The next day the police transported them to the Baisu prison, some kilometres northeast of Mount Hagen town. They were given three months jail sentence from February to their release in May.

PARENTS DIVORCED

This new experience of being in prison was terrible. A bucket for excreta and urine was placed right next to where they slept and ate. They were given very little food to eat by the prison warders. One evening after dinner, Moka and Nii fought each other inside the prison camp over part of an argument that led them to prison.

In order to avoid further problems during the course of their term, the prison officers transferred Moka to Madang prison while the rest including Nii served their terms in Baisu. Since Paraka was assigned the task as a cook in jail, he ate food whenever he felt hungry so he was satisfied at all times. However, his brothers and father were very hungry every day. Paraka thought it was wise to give some food to his father even though he was against him. He did so secretly but gave nothing extra to his brothers. Every time he sneaked food to his father, Nii would assure Paraka that all their problems were going to be solved after they were released from prison. They began to share soap and blankets in prison also. Paraka learnt a lot about human behaviour and recognised that enemies could become friends in prison.

After three months they were released from prison. Lonely clouds drifted across the blue sky as relatives waited outside the prison camp to welcome them home. The duty warder checked the roll and told them to leave. As they left through the open gate, many of the prisoners with remaining years to serve shed tears and waved goodbye.

One of the prisoners, a good friend of Paraka, whispered into his ear. "Pilis brata, noken lus tingting long mi taim yu stap long peles." [Please brother, do not forget me when you are at home.] Paraka promised him, "I know exactly what it's like to be here so don't worry, I surely will remember you." Paraka meant every word of his promise and visited the prisoner.

Hugs, tears and recrimination filled the air. "What if one of us was killed in the fight" Paraka commented. They promised not to quarrel or fight among themselves over land issues or any other related matter in future.

When Paraka returned home he was amazed to find that everything had changed. He had severely degraded the good reputation and positive image that he once possessed because he fought with his brothers and father. All the faith and trust people in the community had in him was eventually withdrawn. The people whom he represented did not value him anymore; instead they saw him as a very aggressive and corrupt leader. He realised that it took ages to build up one's reputation but one can lose that in a very short time. He brooded that his image had been spoilt from doing only one bad thing. His people chose not to remember all the good things that he had once done.

Life was different between the two families after their prison experience. Their father, Nii made sure that they cooperated and took part in any form of ceremony. They had meetings and planned who would do what. For instance, when they exchanged pigs in a moka ceremony, every one of them contributed including their father. Although he was heading towards old age, he had contributed more in terms of pigs and money than the sons in any ceremony. However, they did not appreciate and realise how much he was contributing, taking it for granted until he passed away in December 1989 aged 60. They believed that he died of food poisoning as he was not very old or sick before he died. However, there was no evidence to prove their assumptions, therefore they were unable to take revenge.

The night before he died, he slept alone in his house, while Dawe slept in the women's house. In the morning, Dawe saw that his house was closed so she thought he had woken up early and gone somewhere. She did not bother to check until later during the day when she saw that the door was closed from the inside. She called out to him and knocked very hard on the door thinking that he was still sleeping. Unfortunately, there was no response so she called for a few of her grand children to help her break the door open. When they went to his room, all were shocked to learn that he was dead. His death brought an end to all form of conflict amongst the families.

CHAPTER 10

PIGS, LAND & WIVES

Traditionally, during the pre and post-colonial periods, a leader was viewed as a wealthy man if he had many wives and owned lots of pigs and land.

Paraka had much land but not so many pigs and wives so he thought to himself if I had many wives and pigs then I would be a big man. His decision to marry a lot of women and have many pigs looked after by his women was easy. He searched for young ladies everywhere in the Hagen North area of the Western Highland Province. One day he went to Lumusa, a sub District of the Baiyer District to collect Council taxes. There he met a young lady who caught his attention.

Finally, after some heated eye contacts, he approached the young lady and asked if she would marry him. Finally, she agreed. After collecting taxes, he took her home to Kuipboat where she stayed with Paraka. One day she went to town with Puri on their tractor to sell some vegetables at Mt Hagen. When they returned in the afternoon, Puri told his brother that the lady had an affair with another man while he was busy selling vegetables in the market. Even though, Paraka was comfortable with the idea of polygamy, he knew he would not marry a woman involved with adultery. Puri asked him not to marry her because she had been unfaithful. He took Puri's word, decided not to marry the lady but instead suggested she marry a bachelor by the name of OkoGarmi, also a member of the *Kyakini* tribe. This held no interest for her so she returned to her home. It would be twelve years before his eyes fell on a future wife.

His cousin Tralowa from the Kunyanga tribe was also a councillor at that time. One day Paraka took Tralowa in his Toyota Stout to Tomba, an area in the Tambul Nebilyer district. Upon arriving there, they saw many interesting places and people, but those which captured Paraka's interest were the beautiful young women.

So he said to his cousin, "there are a lot of good looking young women in this place but there are none at our own place."

Tralowa looked at him and with a smile on his face, responded with the suggestion

"If you are interested in marrying one then I could get you one from my place".

Paraka was very pleased at what Tralowa said and they drove home that day remembering his cousin's promise that a lady would visit Paraka's house in a few days. Once at his home Tralowa convinced Traliya that she should marry Paraka and she agreed.

Paraka thought it would be wise to share his desire to marry another women with his wife, Simbu, the first wife of the Ukuni lineage. Simbu was working in their family garden at Ambutoa. Paraka stood some meters away from the garden and whistled at her to go over to where he stood so that he could tell her something.

She was afraid to do what Paraka asked because she thought that he was going to propose they have sex so she quickly said, "the boy is still breastfeeding, what do you want in the middle of this broad day light? "

At that time women believed they would fall pregnant anytime they slept with their husbands so while they were still breastfeeding their babies they refused to sleep with their husbands. This meant that husbands and wives did not have sexual contact for a number of years after the birth of a child.

Simbu already had given birth to two boys Pius who was six and the baby Bruce. She was reluctant to add to her family so quickly and turned away from Paraka to hoe the ground to plant more sweet potatoes.

Paraka understood her reaction so he again called her reassuring Simbu that sex was not what he wanted. When he told her what he did want Simbu disagreed strongly. His cunning soon swayed her to his desire. He pretended to cry, picking up some soil from the garden bed and pretended to swallow while walking way. "Since you do not let me marry another wife I will commit suicide. You will become a widow and then can marry a bachelor". Alarmed at this chain of events, Simbu called her husband back and apologised, consented to his taking a second wife.

That afternoon Simbu and Paraka drove to Traliya's place to collect her.

Custom decreed that before any woman went to the man's place, she must carry a bilum on her head and hold a stick. The bilum symbolised that she would bear children and carry them in it as well as food when required. The stick represented a digging stick that women would use to dig kaukau.

Women were advised not to carelessly leave the stick anywhere. The belief that her marriage to that man was going to be dissolved, or likely that the husband was going to marry some more wives after her if her stick was trodden on was widely held by all.

The relatives of the bride prepared Tralya for Paraka to take her to his place.

Her family roasted two pigs, one for Tralya to take to her groom's place while the second was for her families to eat. Paraka selected a second woman to accompany Tralya to his place to stay for three days while the bride price was negotiated. A cow, thirty kina shells, ten pigs plus $AUD300 Parka paid for his new wife. Tralya settled into her new lifestyle with the advice from her family ringing in her ears. "You must be kind and obedient to your husband and his people. Do not grow greedy. Ignore this advice and your husband is likely to divorce you or take another wife."

Paraka now 29 years old built Tralya a house and gardens as he had done for Simbu.

With so much land left to cultivate, Paraka decided to marry more wives as his two wives could not cultivate all the land or look after all his pigs. In those times and even today, pigs are used as currency for payment in any form of ceremony such as moka, pig killing, bride price, or compensation. Paraka understood that a man who owned many pigs was able to participate in the various ceremonies with his wealth and seen as a leader of the community.

For many years tribal fights between neighbouring tribes dominated a way of life.

The day arrived when the tribes reached a decision to make peace and live together in harmony. In order to achieve that the Kyakini tribe had to pay some compensation for the number of deaths caused by their fighting. A large number of pigs and kina shells was offered by the Kyakini, more than any other tribe could offer, to attract comment and admiration.

To prove to the other neighbouring tribes and the district as a whole that their prolonged conflict had come to an end that, the Kyakini tribe held a week long singsing in traditional costumes. The celebrations were held at Kuipbout, Paraka's moka ground, then at Pulisa, the home of a different faction of the Kyakini tribe.

Before Paraka changed into his traditional costume, he went down to a nearby creek to wash. A widow interested in Paraka followed him to the creek. While he was washing she came over and told him she wanted to marry him. Even though he did not like her he told her that he would see her later.

For the first five days, each group danced in their own respective places. Then on the last day, a Saturday, they all joined together at Pulisa to march around a big moka field. They sang meaningful songs promoting their positive attributes while denigrating the morals of other tribes. Since Paraka was the councillor of the tribe, he led the rest of the men in the march wearing his council badge tied to his forehead. People from far away and nearby came to watch the entertainment. Many people in the audience knew about Paraka's good leadership qualities and respected him. When they saw him leading the march they clapped their hands and shouted acknowledgment of their feelings towards him. His pride soared.

Although he was married with two wives he still looked young so many young ladies focused their eyes on him, not going to him to tell him that they wanted to marry him. At least one of those admirers did not want to go home without asking him to marry her. Paraka was surprised at her approach when she stated "today we will go to your house." He responded, "okay, I'll see you later in the evening after the singsing is over so hang around." Paraka wanted to take her home but he did not want to tell his two wives because they would get angry and fight which he did not want to do in public.

In his cunning way, Paraka played a small trick by calling Simbu and Traliya to him so that he could tell them something. As they stood in front of him, he said "I think there is going to be big fight between our tribe and the enemy tribe because the amount of compensation we paid is not enough. Therefore you two ladies have to go home before it gets dark because it is likely that some of our big men are going to be killed. You must go to your own homes and stay until everything is settled. Take the little children also with you."

They believed what their husband said and went home quickly but saw that everything was as peaceful. The lady who approached Paraka with the request to marry him is Kolga, now his third wife, from the Enga Pin clan of the Kumdi Komonka tribe in the Mul District of Western Highlands Province.

The singsing ended very late in the afternoon. Everyone was busy heading to their respective homes except for Paraka who was still indecisive on whether or not to take Kolga home. Finally he told her "today we cannot go home as you suggested, instead you and your brother can wait for me at Rugli, (a place of the Mul District) and I will come a week from today to take you home to marry you."

The days passed. Still Paraka had not told his two wives of his decision. So the night before he intended to bring Kolga to their homes Paraka spoke with both of them. "Guess what! Tomorrow, I will bring a young lady home to marry her." As soon as they heard that they laughed because they thought he was joking. They assumed that they were going to be his only wives. He had not told them of his intentions to marry many. Therefore they started teasing him as he had anticipated. "If you do bring her home then you are very smart." Paraka then jokingly asked them, "would you two warmly welcome her if I bring her home?' "Yes! We surely will do anything you would like us to do for her if you bring her home," was their positive response.

"Ok! Well, if you two are not upset, can you cook some food for her please?" Paraka begged. Again they both responded, "Yes, we are prepared, we'll buy some rice with the last eight dollars that we have." So Paraka told them, "Alright, I think that is enough so you buy it and have it ready while I go down and bring the lady home."

Kolga and her brother Makinta were waiting for Paraka at Rugli as arranged. They got in his car and drove towards Paraka's home. He dropped both off near the Baiyer District Office and told them to walk to his home, a few kilometers away, while he drove to town to buy food. "The first house on the way is mine. Go in and stay with the two women until I return" he told the surprised couple. When his wives saw the strangers they wondered who they were. Simbu and Traliya did not know Kolga was the young lady he had joked about marrying because they had never anticipated he was going to marry another wife. Instead they guessed that the young man and woman might be visiting relatives. When Makinta finally explained the reason for their visit that Paraka wanted to marry his sister, the wives explained 'oh! So it was you whom our husband wanted us to meet".

Simbu and Traliya warmly invited them into the roundhouse and quickly boiled rice for them. It was common before the white men came, that visitors were greeted with home grown food such as sugarcane and kenga, a special kind of banana. Gradually those foods were replaced by rice, which was regarded as a very special treat.

When Paraka finally arrived home, Simbu and Traliya were relaxed and showed no anger towards the situation. The visitors stayed through the next day when Paraka sent a message to Kolga's relatives to come. He was going to pay bride price of $AUD300, ten pigs, ten kina shells and a cow. They took everything that he gave them except the cow. It was given to Kolga's father but he left it behind because there was no fence around the grazing field. That cow eventually caused friction between father and son when Makinta killed the cow without getting permission from his father who had gown old. Makinta and his men roasted the cow and ate it. He saved a small piece for his father who was very surprised at what his son told him.

At first he disbelieved his son's actions but when he discovered it was true, Kilip cursed his son, Makinta, saying that after he died that he would kill his son. His family thought that it was just a curse and that nothing would happen. But soon after Kilip's death, Makinta suffered from a very long illness where he could not eat. There was something in his throat that stopped him from eating anything at all. He could not even swallow or excrete. So what happened was his food was forced down into the body by using a pipe and the wastage was thrown out likewise. As a result of not eating, he lost a lot of his weight and he was as thin as a stick when he finally died.

Kolga, Simbu and Traliya were cooperative and did everything according to their husband's expectations. He built a separate house for Kolga and made gardens for all the three wives so none of them complained about anything. Only three wives were not enough for him. Despite the pigs and other wealth that he possessed he planned to marry more women so that he could be traditionally viewed as a true leader.

A year after the three wives were settled, he decided to search for a fourth wife. One day as he drove home from town a woman stood by the side of the road at Rugli and stopped his car. He asked what she wanted. She replied that she wanted to go home with him to marry him.

Paraka suspected she was already married. When questioned her response was positive. He felt reluctant to take her home because he knew he would be in trouble for taking another man's wife and at the same time he did not want to upset the husband. However, the lady insisted that she wanted to go with him and leave her current husband, a village councillor from the Kumdi lineage. She was not his only wife; he had several wives like Paraka. When she realised that he was not interested and his decision was final, she asked if he could just give her a lift to her Aunty's place. Paraka was surprised when he found out her aunty was his stepmother, Dawe.

In his hunt to add more wives Paraka heard of one lady from the nearby Kep tribe who had recently married to a man of the Kumdi lineage but soon after the bride price was paid she left her husband and ran away. Her people were very sad and angry because they were happy with the bride price. However, they had to return everything to the Kumdi people. The reluctant bride's father was particularly interested in the two cassowaries he had gained so felt very angry when he lost them.

Paraka decided he wanted to marry this woman so he approached her father with a request for his permission. The father knew about Paraka's marriage to three wives but his response was that as long as he received the same bride price, especially two cassowaries, he could marry his daughter. The next day she came with all her relatives to receive the bride price of two cassowaries, $AUD300, ten pigs and kina shells.

The following year he married Mar't but not formally in terms of giving bride price in public. However, he did give some amount of money and pigs secretly to her relatives. Although he took her as his fifth wife, he still did not trust her, did not build her a house or even make gardens for her. He was afraid that she would leave him at any time. Mar't sensed she seemed to be a burden so she got frustrated with him and the rest of his wives and burnt down the new house that Paraka had built for his third wife. Paraka was furious with what she did and put her in jail at Baisu. While she was there, none of her relatives went to visit her but expected Paraka and his relatives to visit her instead. Mar't stayed in prison for almost a month without anyone visiting her. A few days before her release Paraka decided to go to visit her taking cooked food. As soon as he saw Mar't, he hugged her and pretended to cry because he was afraid that if he did not show her that he cared for her she would run away. Paraka quickly gave her the food that he bought and after she ate it he left her and returned to his home. A few days after he visited, she was released from prison. Her parents and relatives went to the prison to get her but Paraka knew that Mar't was not going to go with them so he stayed at home waiting her arrival by Public Motor Vehicle.

His five wives all had children so he had to cater for the needs of his own family as well as his brothers. Since he was the eldest son he carried the responsibility of paying bride prices for his brother's wives. Although there were so many mouths that he had to feed, he managed to satisfy the various needs. He helped others, If there was a tribal issue of paying compensation or making moka, Paraka always took the lead in getting the biggest amount whether in terms of either pigs or money. The biggest moka made in 1995 involved the Nii family alone who gave the Senapuni tribe 374 pigs and 15,000 kina.

The custom exists that if a leader or family member dies, the tribe of the deceased person's mother had to be given compensation or settlement. Paraka's beloved brother Bill died in his sleep from an unknown illness. His mother Lengame's people received the above because she gave birth to him who later became a very prominent leader. Paraka realised that his decision to marry many wives was a good one because without them he would not have had so many pigs to make moka.

CHAPTER 11

WHITE MEN INTRODUCE LOCAL GOVERNMENT

The introduction of the Local Government Council by the Australian Administrators was a concept foreign to the natives, one in which leaders were elected by the people as opposed to that of the traditional concept of leadership acquired through hereditary and accumulated wealth. It was introduced during the time when Paraka was due to follow his father, uncles and forefathers as the tribe's leader.

He was a man torn between two directions; to follow the traditional path to leadership or accept the modern method descending upon his people who had produced many fine leaders past.

Even prior to Paraka's father's birth, the Kyakini tribe had leaders who earned respect from all the tribes. They were seen as godfathers and feared the most. A fine example was Ale. Paraka was always responsive to the story of Ale because he so wanted to be like him.

Ale was a very wealthy man more so than any other leader that ever lived in Baiyer. He had more than enough of everything including the many wives he married. His influence reached as far as Enga to most parts of Western Highlands Province and within Baiyer. His God-gifted wisdom and ability to predict accurately what was going to happen drew Paraka's interest. If a feast in certain parts of Enga or Western Highlands was being held, he would beforehand foretell and predict that a quarter of meat would be given to him. After a short while, his predictions would be materialised in a piece of meat being brought to him. When that happened, his wives would gather greens and other food to re-roast it because without having it heated they could be sick. When he noticed his wives preparing to heat the quarter of the pork, he would tell them not to do so because the other quarter was still on its way.

"A pig has got so many parts so wait till the other part arrives" he told his wives who listened to him convinced that what he said would happen. It did. The meat was re-roasted and eaten by all.

Ale was highly respected, so much so that once he demanded that a tribal fight should cease, it ceased. Unfortunately, he died of food poisoning. Jealousy was believed to be the motive and his tribesmen were convinced either of the two neighbouring enemy tribes had caused his death. The men of Paraka's tribe fought in retaliation with the enemy tribe killing more of their men than their own. Ale was indeed poisoned by the enemy tribe. It was believed that Ale's spirit was with the Kyakini tribe giving strength and power to the tribe to become victorious over their enemies in the end.

The newly introduced modern concept of leadership was one whereby any interested ordinary members of a particular society could stand to apply. It ignored the qualities of education, the ability to speak fluently in public or to own money. Unlike the traditional past, where only the son of a wealthy man inherited his father's fame or leadership measured by their ability to make moka, owned many pigs, kina shells and money.

At times Paraka felt caught between the old and the new ways taking over his country but he was always optimistic about the future. He felt he could accept such changes brought about by the white men. He lacked education, thought it unlikely that he could fit into the modern idea of leadership but wanted to try while holding on to traditional leadership. He remained puzzled as to which route he should take. Still indecisive about which path to follow, he heard a rumour that the white men were issuing something called Council in Mount Hagen to choose a leader, regardless of whether or not he was one before.

His father and uncle had spent years moulding him to take over as the tribe's leader so Paraka felt the pressure on him to accept the new form of leadership.

However, first of all he wanted to find out what it was like so he and his father decided to go to Mount Hagen. Nii and Paraka took one of Dawe's pigs without her permission and set off on foot for Mount Hagen. When they were tired, they rested under shade since it was a very hot sunny day. The pig's slow walk made Paraka and his father exhausted but they never wanted to give up. After they had rested a little they walked again until they reached Kwinga at nightfall so they spent the night at a friend's house. Early the next morning they woke up even before the birds welcomed the new day with their beautiful choirs, and started walking against the chill. The pig enjoyed the cooler weather and walked a little faster than the day before. Nii and Paraka shivered since they had not brought anything warm enough to defend them against the cold, which penetrated their bones. They had to mentally beat the frost and conquer those shivering moments in order to achieve something that they believed would enlighten their future.

When the sun blazed down on the two men they were already midway between Bukapena, the location of the Mul District Office and their destination. Every time they came across an inviting shade tree, they rested a short while then continued in the hope that they would reach his friend, Pena Uwa from the Jika Mukuka tribe, a traditional leader like Nii, on the same day. Nii had heard that the village leaders who were living around Mount Hagen were assisting in the issue of the council. They were optimistic that their own traditional way of acquiring things, which involved the concept of give and take, would encourage Pena to help them.

The pig was a bribe.

When Pena Uwa saw Paraka and his father arriving at his home, he greeted them with sincere respect. He was surprised at the pig that they took with them and asked, "why and how have you brought the pig with you?"

"We walked all the way from Baiyer with the pig to give it to you so that you could do us a favour" Nii responded.

The response left him in shock because he could never imagine that they could have walked so far with a pig. "So tell me now, what was it that you wanted me to do in return for the pig?" he asked,

Without hesitation Nii spoke. "We have heard that there was something called council being issued by the white men in Mount Hagen. We learnt that you are assisting the white men in issuing it so we came to consult you just in case you knew something about it. If that is true we are offering this pig to you so can you do something in return. Please get a council from the white men and give it to me".

"Yes I will surely get you one" he assured them.

Paraka sighed with relief that their tiring journey full of hungry moments and frost bite had at last paid off. After a warm welcome, Pena invited them to stay the night in his very huge round hausman where he lived by himself. His many wives and numerous children lived in a huge rectangular house divided into sections according to the number of wives. Apart from his other accumulated wealth, he owned a big house in which he kept so many pigs that equalled that of the number of bees in a honeycomb. As they were telling stories, Pena's wives brought cooked and raw food for them. As the night grew late, the overriding power of sleep took hold of the men. Very early the next morning the three men got out of bed before anyone else and without having breakfast doubled their paces hoping to reach Mount Hagen earlier than anyone else. It was quite a long walk from Togoba to Mount Hagen but Paraka and his father were used to walking long distances and so was Pena so they showed no sign of fatigue. Paraka and Nii were very confident that they were going to get the council through Pena since he was their good friend who took their side. The thought of acquiring what seemed to have been the key to being a modern leader encouraged them to walk even faster and they reached Mount Hagen at the time they thought they would.

Fortunately, they were first to arrive at the venue in which the Administrator was issuing the council. With the Administrator were those assisting him with the work. Paraka and his father were strangers to the Administrator so were reluctant to speak to him directly so used Pena as their translator. Paraka stood before the Administrator and pleaded with him saying,

"Excuse me Master, mi pela father harim that you givim something kolim council so mitupela bin interested so walkabout all the way from Baiyer long bai yu givim yumi tupela one."

What he meant was that they had walked all the from Baiyer just to be issued with a council. Even though Paraka spoke broken English with Pidgin that the Administrator understood, Pena Uwa had to relay the message to him because he knew him very well. After listening to their request through Pena, the Administrator hesitantly looked at Nii and Paraka and said "I am very sorry to give you a negative response that you two had not hoped for and that is I will not issue you with one yet. I am still going to give it to you but only if you fulfill some requirements."

Paraka was emotionally ill when he thought about the possible requirements. If one of those was education then he was undoubtedly off the list because he had not received adequate education. To Paraka's disbelief the administrator briefed them that the first requirement was the size of the population of their tribe. He said "it is very important that you have enough people in the tribe that you are going to represent because if I see that there are not enough people, I will simply not give you the council."

The administrator explained.

"And the other thing that anyone has to possess is his capability of leadership. If you satisfy these requirements then you are likely to be given the council.

However that does not mean that if you satisfy these two requirements you will get it; you have to be elected to represent your people."

They listened attentively as he continued.

"There are others who could be contesting for the council also because it's not a one person thing. Any interested person is likely to contest but it depends on the people who they think is capable of leading them. Also any tribe that does not have enough people will have to combine with another tribe which also has the same number of people. Whether anyone tells me verbally that they do have enough people or not, I will not believe it unless I prove it myself after carrying out a census (collecting the names of adults who were capable of voting).

I will go to your place in a week's time and talk to you all more on this matter so go home now and inform all the people in the village about it. You all must meet at a particular place and wait for me. Now that there is nothing else I am going to say, see you two then."

Although Nii and Paraka did not get the council on that day, Paraka was very happy with the requirements, which he believed he could meet to succeed to the council. There were enough people in his tribe and if anyone was going to compete with him, he was optimistic that he was going to succeed because his tribe's people had long ago hoped that he was going to take the place of his father.

If Paraka was to be a traditional leader like his father and other uncles, he would have automatically become one. However, since he had to move along with civilisation, there was doubt as to whether he was automatically going to be leader. The Administrator was clear in his statement that there were others who were going to compete with him. While he tried to accept the white men's rule he did not care about an educated person competing with him. He felt the urge to try rather than to give up which would result in his aspiration of being a reflection of his father and uncles not being fulfilled. This would bring shame on him throughout his society.

After their visit with the Administrator was finished, Nii and Paraka left Mount Hagen to walk back home. They were thrilled they did not have the pig to slow them down but both men brooded about Pena's behaviour. It was shameful of him to get their pig without doing something for them. He had not told them they need not give anything in order to be issued with the council. However, they tried not to think of the pig and kept walking, doubling their pace to reach home by evening.

Both men were tired and hungry and not in any mood for long discussions on their adventure so the family members asked no questions. Nii and Paraka retired to their separate homes instead.

Although the men had not informed anyone about their plan to walk to Mount Hagen, somehow the whole tribe had learnt about it and very early in the morning they gathered at the Hausman in which Nii lived. Paraka joined the group ready for conversation. When Nii told them that they were unsuccessful they all looked down not pleased at all with the news. Everyone who had high expectations on Paraka being the next leader lost all hope because it seemed to them that there was no other way of obtaining it. Nii and Paraka could have lifted their morale by informing them what they were told by the Administrator but they were afraid that the information would leak out which would have been a threat. Both men had agreed not to disclose any more information to the gathering knowing that they would educate them on the day the Administrator was going to come.

Paraka told them about Pena's dishonesty causing all the relatives and family members to feel frustrated with him. They even wished he lived close by so that they could quickly go and bring the pig back to Dawe who was definitely not pleased with them for taking her pig and bringing nothing in return.

Nii and Paraka were impatiently counting down the days until the Administrator was going to arrive in their village to talk to them.

They were dismayed when they learnt from others exactly the same information that they were told by the Administrator. They thought that they had been the only people from Baiyer that went to Mount Hagen. Before the arrival of the Administrator, they learnt that the information had leaked from the Patrol Officer who was advised by the Administrator to remind the people on his behalf, to be prepared for his visit.

When Paraka realised that almost everyone was aware about the council, he was a bit worried he was not going to gain the necessary votes if the people elected someone else. He feared that bribery might be involved, but he constantly reminded himself that he would win the council through his charisma, allure and fascinating behaviour that was admired by almost all of the Kyakini people. With that as a cornerstone, he awaited the arrival of the Administrator with overriding impatience. Some people who had some knowledge about the subject came to him to assure him that they were on his side even if it meant they might lose their lives. Paraka did not publicly let the Kyakini people know that he was intending to contest the election for the council.

All the people who lived in and around Kumbareta gathered there as it was the location the Administrator had chosen for the meeting. People prepared to welcome him in different ways. Some were in traditional dress and danced while others made feast. One of those interested in the council was Raima of the tribe of Traliya. By roasting ten pigs, he indirectly relayed to others that he was an intending contestant. Paraka did nothing. He believed he had done his part by taking the pig to Pena Uwa achieving no reward for his actions.

The Administrator arrived and was warmly welcomed by the huge crowd. Enthralled by the manner in which they reacted to his visit, he stood on the platform that had purposely been built for him to address the interested parties. Two other men from Paraka's tribe were also interested in the contest. Their interests were made known to the public on that day but only Paraka's family knew of his intentions.

The crowd grew silent as the Administrator started his session.

"The first thing you need to know is that the size of the tribe's population will have a bearing as to whether or not there can be a council. The tribe with the bigger population would be successful. Smaller number tribes could combine to gain sufficient numbers to gain a council".

After the murmuring amongst the crowd eased, the Administrator continued.

"There will be a census to find out the names and numbers in each tribe. Next time I come after the census has been carried out, there is going to be an election probably within a month's period". He reminded all the people to make up their minds on whom to vote especially those whom they thought would represent them best. When he returned after conducting the census, they were to vote. After explaining the voting system the Administrator returned to Mount Hagen.

In Paraka's tribe he had three others intending to contest the Council position. Only his father and uncle were complicit in his bid for selection. One day during the campaign a well-respected and feared warrior died. Kyawaleta had fought and conquered land alongside his tribesmen, Nii, Koembo, and Pyapowa. The focus moved from campaigning to Kyawaleta's funeral. Even though in mourning, the three contestants gave speeches at the funeral declaring their intention to stand for the Council.

As the occasion of the funeral had drawn large numbers of people, many of the older men directed the conversation on whom they thought should and should not contest these new elections. Koembo was nominated initially with strong support but eventually opposed because of his very short temper and that he would do anything he wanted if in power. The risk of having the Council taken away as a consequence of misbehaving was too strong. Koembo realised that there was no chance of him winning so he stood before the crowd and yelled, "if I am not going to contest then my son will", his son being in reality his nephew Paraka. So it was confirmed that

Paraka was going to contest the election along with the other two candidates from his tribe.

White man electioneering began. Candidates moved amongst the people attempting to garner all the votes. Paraka kept a low profile because he was convinced that he was going to win in the election. His mother's hope for him to become a powerful leader was about to become a reality. When the Administrator returned to the Baiyer District for the second time to carry out the census he was welcomed by people in traditional costumes, others neatly dressed in their best clothes while the preparation of feasts abounded. Paraka and his supporters did nothing but waited patiently because he had already given away a pig to a man who gave him nothing in return. He wasn't going to be caught twice.

The Administrator arrived at the Kumbwa-Maip tribe first. Men from that village had assisted with carrying the huge, heavy patrol box delivering it to the adjacent village at their border, returning from whence they came. The census showed that the population was not large enough to qualify for a council. Disappointed faces greeted the Administrator when he announced, "sorry, looks like I will not issue your tribe with a council because it is too small. Your two tribes will be combined with the neighbouring Ramoi tribe."

But the leaders of the two tribes did not agree with the Administrator. "That tribe is our enemy. It is an impossible situation. Please give us our own Council." The Administrator stood firm with his decision. When the tribesman pleaded "please, if you do not give us a real council, can you present us with something like this". He held an empty meat tin in his hand. "At least this would satisfy us as long as it is metal and shiny, because we simply cannot combine with the neighbouring Raimoi tribe which is our great enemy."

The Administrator's initial stubborn stance melted so he finally promised to assign a Council to them on his next visit. He had no issue with awarding a Council status to the Kep and Kunyanga tribes as their numbers were sufficient.

WHITE MEN INTRODUCE LOCAL GOVERNMENT

The Administrator travelled on to Kemalipu to carry out the election because most of the people from Paraka's tribe live there, high up on the mountains. Those living down in the Baiyer valley walked up to the election place. Voting started, a preferential system of voting whereby all the candidates who were contesting at least received a vote. After a long day and votes counted, Paraka was not surprised when told that he had won the election. His relatives and supporters celebrated his victory, the Administrator overnighted in the village and continued on his way early the next morning, keen villagers assisting with the patrol box. Paraka showed no disappointment when the winning Council badge was not available, as he felt confident it would eventually arrive, him being such a winner.

It would be three years after he was elected as a Councillor that he received the desired badge. Date December 1968. He was 27 years old. His people addressed him as Councillor Paraka.

The Kiap explained that the Local Government Council was introduced mainly so that local or village people could communicate directly with the government. Councillors were to be mediators between the government and the people. The council and the individual councillor's duty were to maintain, control, and educate their people about the task and importance of the Administration. Above all the most important duty as far as new development was concerned was gathering all able village men and women to help in building roads villages and schools.

After their briefing, all Councillors returned to their various villages to share their newly found knowledge.

Paraka realised for the first time that being a leader meant that he had taken on a lot of responsibilities, not only catering for the needs of his family members but also having to look after the whole tribe. He attended meetings at the Baiyer District patrol office at appointed times, proving a very different approach from accepted traditional leadership. The costs involved in the building of infrastructure were financed directly by the National Government since the Provincial Government had not yet been convened. Each District was allocated $AUD3000 with the Council raising other revenues through imposing taxes on ordinary village people. Newly married couples were charged fees for the registration of their marriage, men paid $6, women $1 while those operating trade stores paid $6 before they could trade. The tribesmen reluctantly accepted this payment of taxes to the white Administrator. Trucks and tractors were bought to complete the work assigned by the Colonial Administrators achieving the aims set by the white man.

In 1968, Paraka was appointed to the finance committee. Within four years Paraka was Council President, presiding over all the councillors of the Baiyer District. He replaced the sacked Council President who attended a council meeting while drunk.

Paraka rose steadily in the political arena, gaining election as a member of the Melpa Area Authority, from 1972 till early 1979 while retaining his position as Baiyer District Council President. His good work of setting up the Kombolpa High School, two additional community schools, plus building a few roads, bridges and an aid post was forgotten when he was sent to prison for fighting with his father and brothers over a land dispute. When Paraka was released in May, other councillors had taken over his positions.

Paraka's other brother Billy Nii also won the 1977 National Election in their Mul-Baiyer open electorate and entered Parliament. However, he was thrown out of Parliament after a court of disputed returns and a by-election was conducted, losing the by-election so he returned to the police force.

CHAPTER 12

WESTERN HIGHLANDS PROVINCIAL POLITICS

Asleep on a bed in the house of an Evangelical group formed by the Australian Baptist Church, Paraka was touched by a vision. A man stood in front of him stretching out his right hand and said "Paraka! I am giving it to you, please take it." At a snail's pace he woke up feeling drowsy and threw his right hand in the hope of receiving something from the stranger. To his astonishment after regaining full consciousness, he discovered that what he saw and heard was only a dream. Still sitting there not knowing what to do next, he peeped through the tiny holes of the walls, woven bamboo stalks, to learn that it was still dark outside. Next, he closed he eyes and prayed to the lord saying, "Lord! Supposing that this dream has been given by you, please make sure that my mother also sees what I have seen. Amen."

The night's darkness faded as the early morning fog and dew began to cover the whole Baiyer valley. Paraka woke the rest of the men by singing a song and together they left for a prayer meeting at the 'power house' where the evangelists claimed they received power from God. It was believed that if they did not go to the 'power house' they would not win many souls to the Christian faith. Paraka had joined them after his return from prison and was actively participating in the work of God.

They sat in a circle facing each other holding one another's hands getting ready to pray, when Paraka told the little congregation about the dream he had. They interpreted it in their own way and concluded that the Lord was going to give him some kind of blessing. He was advised to prepare himself to receive those blessings. When the prayer meeting ended he went home to find out whether or not his mother had the similar dream. He was very surprised to hear that she did but in her case she saw the man handing him something that looked like a parcel. He believed strongly that the dream had come from God. Paraka prayed earnestly day and night for some time asking God to reveal to him what the dream was about.

Eventually he accepted that God wanted him to lead the all the people of the Western Highlands including the Baiyer District. He politely explained to the evangelists that he was leaving them to contest the election. "Please pray ardently for me as I campaign" as he departed for his home. Armed with only his power of words, his previous experience as a guide for his people, he grew more confident that he would successfully challenge Kundi Maku, the sitting member for Simu-Sip constituency. The year was 1980; Paraka was 41 years old.

The Western Highlands Provincial Government was formed after the National Government had handed down the Provincial Government charter on the 21st October 1978. Previously, there was the Melpa Area Authority where Paraka had been a member. Once the charter was handed down existing members of the Melpa Area Authority automatically became the members of the Interim Provincial Government.

It was the custom of the Kyakini tribe that before the whole tribe took part in any activity such as pig killing, pig exchange ceremony, bride price payment, compensation payments or tribal fights, members of the tribe were required to meet secretly to discuss their actions.

As such Paraka secretly called the men together in a particular place the day before he paid his nomination fee. Women, children and visitors were not welcomed at the meeting. Paraka stood up and broke the silence by saying, "Good evening every one, it is a pleasure to have you all here. I welcome you all to this meeting. You are all aware that the first Western Highlands Provincial Government election is going to be held in three weeks' time. I called this meeting to inform you that I am intending to contest in the election. We cannot be slaves under the leadership of a man from another tribe. Our forefathers and fathers always won so now it is our turn".

Murmuring rose from the crowd as smoke drifted slowly away from the fire embers.

"It will be shameful if we lose this election. I want to hear your views before I go ahead and pay the nomination fee tomorrow. Each of you will have the chance to speak".

At first Paraka was pleased with the overall response to his call for support until a man stood up and said, "Brother, I think you should resign from being a councillor if you contest the provincial elections. Any one of us can take up the councillor responsibilities".

"I think you are right in that," Paraka replied.

The rest of the men were adamant that Paraka remain as a councillor in case he did not win the current contest. When he finally agreed with their argument, the meeting ended and all returned to their respective homes.

The next day dawned sunny and fine, a good omen cried the old and wise tribe members. All the tribesmen lined up and began marching enthusiastically all the way to the District Office. Upon arrival, Paraka paid the nomination fee of fifty kina, as Councillor Peyle Maku of the Troepo tribe authorised his payment. The waiting tribesmen then walked back home secure in their belief that their man would win. The manner in which Paraka's tribesmen had marched to the District Office to have his nomination fees paid communicated a special message to the general public. Firstly, it showed that he had support from within his own tribe and secondly, it meant that he was capable of giving a good challenge to the seating member.

Paraka started campaigning openly but found it extremely hard to convince the people to vote for him through his various policies. People were not educated enough to understand and decide whom to vote for by judging the different policies of each candidate.

Instead they were prepared to support only their own wantoks from the same tribe, clan, language group and so forth, regardless of how convincing the policies of the other candidates were.

The vast majority of the people of Simu-Sip constituency took every activity that led to the election personally. As head of families, fathers would force the wives and children to vote for their candidates. If a member of a particular family refused to vote as directed by the father, there were often fights and quarrels between the father and the rest of the family members.

This also occurs in modern times. It is not only the father's interest, but the community's interest as a whole to take into consideration when voting. If a family votes against the interest of the whole community, civil war would likely break out between the family concerned and the community. Injured parties in such a war would claim compensation from the candidates because it was their fault that caused the fighting. As a candidate Paraka received claims of compensation from injuries, requests for financial assistance to pay for bride price, school fees even though many thought it unfair to burden their candidate with such demands.

Bribery was very common in the highlands.

However, the candidates who distributed bribes did not usually win them because the people had already been given whatever they needed. In Paraka's case, he knew that bribing people on some occasions like he did was an offence but he had to force himself to do it because people had wanted their votes to be bought. "We want something in return for our votes because once you are in power, you won't consider us any more", they repeatedly told him. Such a mentality was a way of life in most parts of Papua New Guinea.

As Paraka did not have enough money to satisfy the accumulated demands by the population of his constituency, he had to travel to all parts of the constituency giving public speeches where he endeavoured to encourage his people to give him a mandate to work for them. Paraka also had so much support because he had previously established a good name by being a Council President and a member of the Western Highlands Interim Provincial Government.

Others hungry for power cheated the people of their constituency promising the voters that as soon as they won the elections, they would abolish the existing Council Head Taxes that was in place at that time. They also promised to pay some kind of a pension to every individual in the constituency as done for the Australia Colonial Administrators.

The candidates knew that it would be difficult to achieve such things. They deliberately deceived the people with their empty promises to get their votes so they could win. Paraka was counting down the number of days until election. The campaign days meant sacrifices of material resources such as pigs, money and food.

Finally, the day came for the polling to take place. Unlike modern times where polling is conducted all over the Province on the same day, at that time there were different polling areas held over different days. For Paraka's constituency the polling began at Kaleponga, an isolated remote place of the Supanyi tribe where there was no road linking to the main road. Some of Paraka's supporters, especially men, went there a day before the polling started to stay for the night.

The final polling was held in his own area at Kuipbout. When the election was over, the scrutineers from Paraka's side came with the tally of votes in his favour. He had received more votes than the others so he was expecting to win.

When a rival candidate was declared winner with only 26 extra votes confusion spread quickly. An investigation found that the rival candidate's tribesmen had bribed the presiding officer by offering him a young woman. In return for the exceptional offer, the presiding officer filled in extra ballot papers for the rival candidate thereby declaring him the winner. Paraka was shocked by this and not at all pleased with what had happened but was declared the runner-up.

Paraka's younger brother John, also upset by the situation said to him, "Brother, since there seems to be an assumed foul play, can we relay the matter to the attention of the Electoral Commissioner?" In response to his request of taking the matter to court Paraka said to John, "winning through court disputes or any other means cannot be seen justified in the eyes of the rest of the population. Whether or not the winner and his supporters have cheated us, it is up to them. If we do win by a very bigger number of votes than just the 26 that they won within the next election, it would mean that they have cheated us." John agreed with his response. Paraka remained confident that he would win the second election because he believed in the dream that he had. As a faithful Christian he waited patiently for the next election period to arrive.

For almost five years after Paraka lost his first election he stayed at home as a subsistence farmer and a village councillor. In the year 1984, writs were issued and he paid his nomination fees to contest the second Western Highlands Provincial Election. The other intending candidates and the seating member also paid their fees.

As the campaign progressed it was obvious that the seating member had lost most of his support. He had failed miserably to fulfill the promises that he made to the people. He did not stop the collection of Council Head Taxes nor had he fulfilled led his promise of the provision of pension to the whole population of the Simu-Sip Constituency. More importantly, he had not brought any infrastructural development to the areas he represented. Paraka loomed high in their expectations and some support was diverted his way.

After having learnt their lesson of voting for the wrong person to represent them in terms of fulfilling their promises, the various tribesmen impatiently awaited the second election so that they would vote for someone capable of delivering goods and services without delay.

Tradition remains in the Western Highlands and the highlands region as a whole that candidates of other tribes or clans are not expected to enter another's tribal boundary. If anyone is seen entering another's tribal boundaries, they are chased away. However, if they persistently go and as a result manipulate and bribe opposing candidates' people, tribal fights flare afterwards if that candidate loses.

When Paraka campaigned the whole day with his supporters in the territory of the Miki tribe in which Yalu was the contestant, they were too tired to return to their own homes. They decided to stay the night at the house of a supporter who was from Yalu's tribe. The man's wife boiled some rice while all the men including Paraka, were talking. Some moments later, a man stood in the dark and yelled out "Hey! Who are those men talking too much inside? When I am contesting, I am not expecting you guys to come and campaign like that in my territory You are out of bounds. You must be man enough to have guts to come to my territory".

The owner of the house signalled them to be quiet so they lowered their voices. Paraka broke out in a pool of sweat and began shivering. He knew he was in the wrong because he should not have gone to another contestant's territory.

Yalu was very frustrated at them for not responding so he walked straight in to the house. His gang, fully armed, waited outside prepared to attack if anything went wrong inside the house. Yalu quickly lifted the pot of rice, which was still boiling on the fire and poured it on the bare back of an elderly man called Pambowa, from Paraka's tribe. Some of the hot grains landed on Paraka's back also. He quickly removed his shirt but his tribesman was not so fortunate. Some of the hot grains of rice got stuck between his waist and the bark belt that he was wearing. "Oh, it's hurting!" cried Pambowa aloud. In retaliation, he grabbed his axe to strike Yalu dead when Paraka whispered, "do not do anything please Father. He was too violent because he knows that we are definitely going to win this election".

Paraka and his men remained still, not reacting at all to Yalu's behaviour. They were aware of the men outside waiting for a reason to attack. Since there was no revenge taken, Yalu felt embarrassed at his words and actions and disappeared with his men. After a fitful night's sleep, Paraka rang his younger brother, Bill, the Provincial Police Commander in the Enga Province and reported the incident that had happened the previous night. Policemen arrived, arrested Yalu and took him to jail.

The seating member had cheated him in the first election but Paraka did not expect him to repeat his treachery in the second election. However, Paraka was wrong. His chief opponent formed a gang and planned their strategy.

The whole population was at the Tinsley Hospital voting place when a sudden fight broke out. Everyone, including Paraka's supporters were confused with what was happening, The gang grabbed the box of ballot papers and threw it on to a waiting well-conditioned Toyota stout and drove away at a very high speed towards the District Office.

Most of the votes belonged to Paraka. As the gang had pre-planned, there was a vehicle waiting mid-way between the district office and Paraka's village with an extra ballot box papers marked with the seating member's name. Their intention was to swap the boxes.

To their misfortune however, something miraculous happened as they neared Paraka's home, which was mid-way between the polling area and where the other truck was waiting. The Toyota Stout lost two tyres to punctures. The vehicle was stuck. The men hoisted the ballot box and began to run towards the place where the second land cruiser was waiting.

Paraka's men ran after them and wrangled the box from the gang, badly injuring the men who carried the box. In their anger the successful men wanted to take on the whole tribe of the seating member but Paraka disliked their idea and directed them not to do so. Paraka's men took the box to the District Office.

On the way they saw the land cruiser waiting to collect the illegal votes. Paraka felt it was a miracle that they had defeated his enemy and was convinced that God had chosen him to be the leader of the people of Simu-Sip and Western Highlands.

The polling at Tinsley was the second last place, so on the next day it was Kuipboat, his village. Counting was held at the District Office where he was declared the winner with 485 extra votes. He entered the Western Highlands Provincial Assembly a proud and determined man to help his people.

CHAPTER 13

WESTERN HIGHLANDS POLITICS

A brand-new land cruiser drove in from the main road towards Paraka's home in Kuipbout. Mr Kaugel Koroka, the People's Democratic Party leader in the Western Highlands Provincial Assembly, stepped out of the car. He had won his Lower Kaugel constituency seat and was searching for winning members from all over the province to form a government in the Western Highlands Provincial Assembly.

"Good morning Mr Koroka, how are you today?" Paraka greeted him warmly.

"I am fine, thank you and how about yourself?" he asked.

"Well, I am fine also and was expecting you anyway," he replied.

As Paraka was a member of the People's Democratic Movement (PDM) he knew Mr Koroka. His visit came as no surprise.

"I came to ask you to form a government in the Western Highlands Provincial Assembly. I must admit to you all gathered here, tribesmen and women alike, that the safety of Mr Paraka is guaranteed while he spends the next few days waiting to form government." Expectation that a losing candidate might appear at any time to kill his winning opponent ran high. Nentepa, Paraka's younger brother got up and asked.

"Mr Koroka, can you promise us that you will give him a Ministerial Portfolio, please."

"I know, Mr Nii is a very strong man in the People's Democratic Movement Party and he deserves one," was his reply.

Some moments later Paraka and Mr Koroka climbed into his vehicle and departed for Mount Hagen. On the way they discussed various issues, both enjoying the trip. Both were winners.

Close to Mount Hagen Paraka turned to Mr Koroka and said, "Mr Koroka, you promised my people that you were going to give me a ministerial portfolio, if that is so can you give me the Minister for Local Level Government Council? I have been a councillor for fourteen years and I know I will perform well in that area."

His reply was, "do not worry about that, you will be a father of the government we are going to form." Mr Koroka assured him.

They did not stop at Mount Hagen but kept on driving towards the highway leading to Wabag. "Where are we going?" Paraka asked.

"We are going to Minimb, the home of Paias Wingti, the father and founder of the People's Democratic Movement Party" Mr. Koroka replied.

On their arrival at Minimb. Paraka met Mr Wingti and the other winners from various constituencies within the province. Tight security surrounded the residence. No one of the assembled group had been informed of what was going to happen. Many felt confused.

Mr Koroka gathered them together and briefed them of the protection due to the possibility that those candidates who lost in the elections would feel jealous and try every possible way to harm those who won.

He then informed them, "in the morning every one of us is going to Sepik. We will go by truck to Enga Province and catch a plane from Wapenamanda airport. Please get yourselves prepared tonight." Mr. Wingti had already left for Port Moresby., the capital of Papua New Guinea.

Very early on a Friday morning the newly elected councillors were awoken by the horn of a 25 seat-bus that was waiting outside to take them to Wapenamanda airport. Grabbing their personal effects, each man rushed to their destiny.

Once seated on the privately booked plane, each man gazed out the window at the scene below. Houses looked like tiny ants squatting beside the road. Paraka stared in amazement at the huge snake that lay beside the valley with the morning sunlight perfectly reflected at its surface. Paraka asked Yuants Kaman, the member for Minj constituency, who was sitting beside him the question.

"Brother, what is that shiny thing that is reflecting the sunlight?" He replied, "come on you should know. That is your place, the Baiyer Valley and the long shiny thing is the Baiyer River."

"I am sorry brother, I did not recognise it," was his quiet reply.

After flying through the wild rugged mountains for several hours, the pilot lowered the plane to land at Wewak airport. They were met by their accommodation bus driver who drove them to their destination. They stayed for a week during which time they visited all of the East and West Sepik Provinces. The group was then flown back to Mount Hagen, not to their respective homes, but all taken by bus to Minimb.

The Government of the Western Highlands Provincial Assembly was formed by the People's Democratic Movement party by a majority of twenty-two members headed by the leader of the party, Mr Kaugel Koroka. On the 4th of July some days later Mr. Koroka was elected Premier for the Western Highlands Provincial Assembly, he began appointing other ministers of his cabinet. Finally, he called out to Paraka saying, "Mr Paraka Nii, I appoint you the Minister for Local Level Government Council.

I know that you understand a great deal about how the local government system in the province functions."

With enthusiasm he replied, "Thank you Honourable Premier Kaugel Koroka, I swear I will serve the people of my constituency and the province as a whole to the best of my ability, given the availability of funds."

When Paraka returned to his village after a month's absence with mixed feelings. His tribesmen and women were all ecstatic that he would lead them but his thoughts that he held little education for such a responsible position troubled him often. His positive attitude would attack his negative fears reminding himself that the lack of education was not an obstacle because the secretaries were going to do most of his writing. His job was only to direct and talk and he did that well. He worked diligently to gain funds for his district. Two community schools gained extra classrooms, roads were built and three bridges finished during this period. In his wisdom he recognised that bringing about infrastructure development was of little importance if the community was not peaceful. Tribal fights were a hindrance to development according to Paraka's view. When a potential conflict arose between two tribes or clans he quickly paid compensation to avoid many deaths as was the case in many other parts of the province. His people were impressed at his initiative to give away big pigs and large sums of money to stop any conflict allowing peace and harmony to reign.

Life moved along steadily until a motion of no confidence by the opposition was cast against Mr. Koroka. On 9th April 1985, two thirds of the Assembly voted for change. Paraka had served for only eight months.

He remained in opposition until writs were issued in May 1988 for the third Western Highlands provincial elections. Paraka paid his nomination fees to contest in the election as usual. His political rival followed his usual behaviour with dirty plans to jeopardize the peaceful election. Fortunately, their plans failed badly. Paraka was declared the winner for the second time with 501 extra votes.

His rival came second, not accepting that result well. He bribed some of Paraka's tribesmen and relatives to burn down all his houses. They burnt down his new round house that Paraka purposely built to accommodate visitors during the election, throwing flames into the new trade store of his first-born son, finishing with destroying a few others of his houses at his village.

Paraka was with Mr. Koroka waiting to form government when news reached him of the fires. All involved including Paraka's cousins were sent to jail. His reaction on hearing this disturbing news was the following. "That's ok, we built the houses with our own hands and we will still build them. Please make sure the men sent to jail are released. There is no point in putting the men into jail when we have already won the election." The men felt great relief and admiration for Paraka as they walked free.

Pleased with his election win, Paraka felt torn between his loyalty to Mr. Koroka and the PDM to form a government; and his younger brother John Nii who believed that Mr. Philip Kapal, leader of the National Party, had the majority of members and was likely to form government. Paraka plus two other elected members from the Baiyer district, Napil Kuri (Lumusa) and Makop Tepoka (Ukuni-Mapowa) were locked inside Mr. Koroka's residential area in Mount Hagen, protected by tight security as usual.

John Nii wanted these three men to join Mr. Kapal so he kidnapped them driving through the locked gate in his land cruiser breaking it. He took the three of them in his car to the Kunai Hotel in Banz.

Mr. Kapal and his other members greeted the three new members warmly. A few days later, the group broke into two lots; one on a bus to Madang, the other to travel to Lae. Paraka stood back waiting to learn which of the two buses Mr Kapal boarded then joined him.

On their way to Lae, Mr Kapal got drunk on beer. Paraka knew that he would promise him a ministerial portfolio while he was under the influence of beer so he asked him, "Mr Kapal you are aware that

I am a strong man of the People's Democratic Movement Party. It will be a disgrace if you do not give me one ministerial portfolio." Mr Kapal responded to him in a very positive manner. "Don't worry, Mr Nii, I will definitely give you whatever you ask for."

On the 4th of July, 1988, Mr Kapal was elected as the Premier for Western Highlands. Paraka was again appointed as the Minister for Local Government Council.

While he served as a Minister, he tried his best to achieve something for his people of the Simu-Sip constituency and the Western Highlands Province as a whole. He gained funds to build four aid posts, some small feeder roads that lead to the main Baiyer road, churches and water supplies. In addition, he took an agenda to the Assembly where he proposed a hundred more council badges be issued throughout the province especially to those tribes that had not been recognised during the colonial period. The Assembly approved and the hundred councils were issued through either the process of elections or appointment. He argued strongly for financial support for Local Government. As a result the Provincial Government budgeted twenty thousand kina (K20,000) every year for the provincial Local Government Council. He celebrated his achievements with a feast on 2 November 1989 killing 200 pigs and roasting them at Kuipboat. He was 50 years old.

>   During this period of my uncle's life, I was facing my fears about school.
>
>   Enrolling at School that time was done not by looking at the ages but through inspection of the natural appearance, the body demeanor and a child's ability to show cause that they were ready to learn.
>
>   In 1987, I was brought to Sikisa community school by my parents to get enrolled. The board chairman, Mali Kuingapu, who was from my grandmother Lengame's Senapun tribe, told me to touch my left ear by my right hand over my head. Seeing that I was unable to do as he advised, he told my parents that I was too small or was not ready to enroll so we

returned home. However, next year at the 9 years of age I was finally enrolled at Sikisa, direct into grade one without any elementary or prep education. It was like feeding an infant adult food but somehow, I managed to grasp things along the way.

My father Puri Nii had built the school in 1974 after appreciating that through education the fabrics of a primitive society would change to avoid a violent clash of cultures. Students came mainly from the neighboring tribes and in my class 15 or so were males with only five females.

Girls' education at that time was restricted by culture and tradition because they were seen only as child-bearing machines, the ones to look after pigs, make gardens and prepare delicious meals for their husbands.

I was 9 years old when I had a quarrel with William Konga from the neighboring Senapun tribe, disputing the ownership over a piece of chalk. I bite off one of his fingernails in my frustration but later we became good friends.

In my first year of schooling, I learned the Alphabet, consonants and vowels, and was able to spell the names of my parents and my own. We studied subjects such as English, Maths, Science and Social Science. In our lunch breaks we played baseball, soccer and village games.

While I was progressing through my school studies my Uncle Paraka travelled with other provincial members to Asian countries visiting Singapore, Thailand and Philippines for a month. "Where do you all come from?" the people asked them with a surprised looks on their faces inferring they had never seen such people like them before. When they answered Papua New Guinea they were met with inquisitive looks. "Well, where is Papua New Guinea, then?"

Paraka felt so embarrassed by their lack of awareness of his beautiful country that he moved quickly away from those in front of him. The size of the population living in the major cities in each of these countries surprised and amazed him.

In 1992 change hit Paraka once more. The National Government suspended the Western Highlands Provincial Government removing all the members from their offices.

They remained suspended until the elections that were held in January, 1995. Paraka contested that election and won for the third time. Although there were many educated and wealthy contestants, the people of the constituency liked and voted Paraka into the Assembly for the third time where he was appointed the Provincial Minister for Health on the 20 January, 1995. After a short period of six months, the National Government abolished the Provincial Government system throughout the country.

CHAPTER 14

PUBLIC SERVICE

From 1964 through 1997 Paraka Nii served as a councillor of the tribe unopposed. Change arrived in the form of two members of his Kyakini tribe in the election held that same year.

I was home for school holidays when a large gathering met at Kuipboat. People were verbally shouting at each other. One of the opposing candidates pointed his fingers at Paraka and yelled across the heads of those staring at him.

"We're tired of your leadership". Turning to face the crowd he demanded that the people not vote for Paraka. After a shot while the second candidate sent abusive words in Paraka's direction. Castrol Lapun Gaiyer, Paraka's maternal cousin, reacted to the aggravated manner in which the two were campaigning. He shouted "brother, the manner in which you campaign signified that of an uncivilised Baiyer who does not really understand the full definition of democracy. "You better go back to school and read what campaigning is all about". Paraka rose to interrupt his enthusiastic relative, pleading with him to say nothing more.

The surrounding atmosphere grew tense. Fighting between the various support groups was highly likely so Paraka took charge.

"I forgive both candidates for all bad comments made against me. Brother you can say and make such comments about me but I will never be moved nor touched by such evil conceived remarks. Remember the Proverb, you can ride a horse into a creek but you cannot force it to drink".

Translation: One cannot change the minds once they decided on whom they wished to vote.

As night settled over the crowd, they began to disassemble in small groups to their respective homes.

Small boys were not allowed at the night meeting prior to the start of voting for the upcoming election. Paraka was meeting with his brothers at Kontopeng, a village still part of the Kyakini tribe, where two of his wives Kolga and Traliya lived.

For security reasons the meeting was moved to Paraka's prayer ground at Haikena kaou. Under the cover of darkness, I crept close to the bushes, tip-toeing like a mouse to make sure I would not be seen. Quietly I settled near the building's rafters. I looked up and my eyes met those of my uncle Kaia Mel. Trepidation shivered through my body at being discovered but he looked away, allowing me to feed my curiosity.

Prior to the commencement of the proceedings, Pastor Kiap from the local church opened the meeting with a prayer. Almost immediately, Puri and Moka, two of Paraka's brothers, stood up expressing their discontent about the manner in which the rival candidate had falsely accused Paraka with negative comments.

Paraka thanked the two brothers for their concern and offered this advice to the gathering. "A leader is someone who accepts criticisms and defeats. He should be the one who loves all his tribesmen and the one who is at the center of peace. A leader is the one who is always at the front of every battlefield trying to mediate peace between the rival tribes. Remember, a leader is someone who can sacrifice all his last savings just to save the unfortunates".

The mood of the meeting lifted as the men in general agreed with Paraka's comments. His brothers were slow to adjust to the wisdom offered but finally capitulated.

Important discussions went on until the early morning hours but I fell asleep around midnight. Voting was due to commence at 8am. When I woke up the next morning I noticed that everyone else had vacated the house and I was the one that was locked inside. Since I was reaching teenage years then, I did not want to miss out on my first time of voting.

I broke open the wooden bark at the side of the rafter and ran home to Marinjapeta, a village a few kilometres from Kuipboat, to be welcomed by the empty house and our three dogs. Everyone else had gone to Kuipboat to cast their vote. I quickly found the key in its hiding place, dressed in my best cloths for the occasion and went to Kuipboat. To my surprise I noticed that there was a big crowd of people gathered in front of Paraka's third wife, Mapa's house. I was undoubtedly convinced that it was the voting venue. I joined the people already in the queue waiting to cast their votes. My excitement at voting for the first time was dampened when Paraka leaned towards me and said "son, you are only sixteen years old and you are not eligible to vote".

The winner of the election was declared at the same venue straight after the voting ended. It was again no surprise as Paraka returned his post with more than three quarters of the votes. Happiness spread itself across every one of his supporters' faces. Victory songs began to fill the humid air.

On the other hand, the minority of the Kyakini faction that supported the rival candidate slowly swallowed their botched pride and dispersed carrying their disconcerted thoughts with them. It was a vivid lesson to observe the two varying responses on the faces of the people; one filled with joy, the other smothered in sadness.

When Paraka was formally declared the winner, he called all his supporters to gather around him to convey his thanks and gratitude to those who had prayed to the Lord for a fair and honest leader so that all the Kyakini people would enjoy the benefits of good leadership. He reassured all his tribesmen that the Lord the God of Moses, Abraham and Isaac is a God that does not let his people down. He believed that the lord had heard the cries of the people for a good leader, and consequently the lord had helped him retain his seat.

One day during his usual trips around the community, Paraka went to Endemarn, the village of the neighbouring Senapun tribe to pay his visit to a man who had been his mentor, Gaiyer Kumba, his maternal uncle aged in his late 90's. His eyes were already blind and could not see properly but could easily identify people by their voices. Since his old legs were shaky, he slowly stood up with the support of a walking stick, easily recognising Paraka's voice and called out, "at last here comes my son. I did not expect that you would come. Your coming is a blessing to me".

With hot tears rolling down, Paraka leaned closer and hugged Gaiyer close to his chest. For Gaiyer, it was a happy moment because he knew that at last the young boy he had raised after the parent's separation had become a great ruler for the people of the Kyakini tribe.

Tears swelled behind his eyes as Paraka heard Gaiyer say to him "Son, I'm going to die as a happy man because I have lived my life and I have enjoyed almost every moment of my life. You are the greatest son I have ever raised. If it wasn't for me, you would not have come this far. I thank God that through the power of his glorious work, He has chosen you to take the reign of the Kyakini people and the District and the Province. You will deliver your people from hardship such as Biblical Moses of Israel did with his people. You will become the Modern Moses of the Baiyer people. I am very proud of you and bless you to continue serving you people".

After such an emotional speech, Paraka thanked Gaiyer for everything that he had done in moulding him to come so far. As daylight faded, Gaiyer's elder daughter Susan brought sugarcane from her garden. More hours were spent telling stories while chewing sugarcane till Paraka left for his home.

Two weeks after Paraka's visit, Gaiyer Kumba passed away peacefully. His funeral was held over two weeks at Lokai Kaoyusa, a village of the Senapun tribe. Paraka and his tribesmen attended the funeral, contributing kind and cash to the immediate families of the late Gaiyer Kumba.

After Paraka's condolence speech, Castrol Lapun, Gaiyer's younger son thanked Paraka and his men for showing their heartfelt concern at the time of sorrow, also thanking people from the other neighbouring tribes that attended the funeral. After two weeks a big feast was held with Paraka offering a pig. He was officially part of the group that was there from the first day of the mourning until the last day, then the feasting day.

Such a feast is customarily held in most parts of the Baiyer society to officially end the mourning period. Relatives of the deceased can then forget about their loss to concentrate on their daily lives.

Paraka served with commitment to his people and the District. He was exclusively involved in the needs of the community, whether that was for a Moka ceremony, pig killing, bride price, compensation or any other needs that involved the pride of the community. He was seen as the orator in terms of peace negotiations between rival tribes and the one who took the lead by contributing the highest amount of money to settle any social disputes.

CHAPTER 15

COUNCIL PRESIDENT

In 1987 the concept of a Council President was introduced to society. Paraka was Minister of Local Level Government Council in the Provincial Assembly at that time and was offered the position of President.

However Paraka instinctively recognised that it was unwise and egocentric to retain both political positions so he decided to offer the Presidency to a councillor, willing to serve the people with pride, honour and dignity. Mr. Goiya Asimbi of the Tralya tribe accepted the Baiyer River Local Level Government Council President post holding that position for two terms.

When the Provincial Assembly system was abolished in 1995 by the Government of Papua New Guinea through an amendment in the Organic Law on Provincial and Local-Level Government, every councillor in each ward area was given more mandates to exclusively carryout their task. The local population began to realise that councillors were just as important as the former Provincial Assembly Members.

Two years after the former Provincial Assembly system was abolished, writs for the Local-Level Government Council throughout Papua New Guinea were issued.

Candidates started campaigning. Paraka worked to retain his seat winning with more than three-quarters of the total votes. His focus then changed to gaining the Council President position. However, due to failure in capital, logistics and man power, Paraka finished the runner up polling 22 councillors to 27. Paraka accepted his defeat magnanimously, returning to his home still to acclaim from his supporters.

Paraka waited patiently for the 2002 elections. When he won as Councillor by more than three quarters of the votes, his thoughts again turned to the longed for Presidency.

All his opposing candidates for the Local-Level Government President seat for Baiyer campaigned very hard. Paraka took all his councillors away from Baiyer to camp in an isolated place.

His strategies did not work, losing by one vote. When he was met with loved ones full of sorrow at his loss, he tried to pacify them by saying "it is a master game, where one has to lose and one has to win. We will try again in 2008". Winning and losing was not new to Paraka as he had survived both over time as the Member for Simu-Sip Constituency in the former Western Highlands Provincial assembly.

In the village of Mandakimb high in the Kontopeng Hills, Paraka worked at planting hectares of coffee, distributing the land equally to his four wives. Mart his fifth wife received no grant as she contributed no work to the clearing of the land being absent in Porgera in the Enga Province for many months. His other wives demanded Mart receive no plot of land and in honouring their request, Paraka knew deep in his heart he would build a new garden for his love somewhere in future.

When Mart returned from Porgera to learn that she had no plot of land in the new area, she was filled with anger and frustration and left for Port Moresby where she stayed for a year with her uncle.

As a first year law student I was strolling through the Gordon's Market in Port Moresby when my Aunt Mart called to me. "Paul come and join your relatives".

As I approached, she came forward and hugged me saying "na tepanum ken popogl eterm ela ya hurr ni ka, ambo ralep woa nomba molanga kelya" in the Melpa language of the Western Highland Province. Translation: she was fed up with her husband for such a bias polygamous treatment and fled to Port Moresby and would not go home. After our conversation, she gave me a fifty kina (K50) and said "this money is for you to buy soap, pen and any other essential items that you may need in school. I do not want you to buy alcohol or lure young girls with this money". I thanked her enthusiastically for giving me the money and we dispersed shortly thereafter.

Eventually Paraka made a new garden for Mart near Tramalau, an area few kilometres from Kuipboat, wooing Mart back into his arms. She was satisfied and happy that her husband had not let her down when she saw that the size of her garden was bigger than that of the other wives. She believed that her husband must have loved her more than any of his other wives to be given the biggest plot of land separate from the other wives. She visited her garden daily keeping busy to ensure no weeds invaded her marvellous garden.

Happiness came easily to Paraka when he saw that his wives had plenty of food to eat, that he was able to share his worldly goods with others in need and his wives supported his actions.

Life was not so easy in his political world. Bribery, conspiracy and hijacking were used to kidnap and force councillors to vote against Paraka for the role of President in the 2008. When his rival candidate observed the flow of support to Paraka, he dropped a new Toyota land cruiser in front of Mr Iki Traima of the Traliya tribe to buy his vote. That was no surprise to Mr. Traima because the night prior to his council election, rumours had speculated that intending candidates for the president seat would drive to any winning councillor's house to hijack them. When Mr Traima, grasped the gravity of the situation, he approached the bribing candidate sitting in the land cruiser assuring him of his support and that he would go to his camp.

Iki's father had been a close friend of Paraka since childhood, often exchanging gifts to strengthen their ties. Because of the close connection between the two men, Iki knew his allegiance would remain with Paraka for the President's vote. Iki quickly pulled Marko, his fellow Tralyia tribesman close to him and quietly told him to take his bag filled with his clothes to Kontopeng, where Paraka was camping with his councillors while Iki pretended to mingle with his supporters. At dusk, he walked all the way to Kontopeng where he was welcomed by Paraka and his supporters.

Meanwhile, the rival candidate who offered a vehicle as a bribe, waited impatiently until he heard that Iki was at Paraka's camp. He had lost round one but had other devious plans in place to ensure he would become the next President. All attempts to hijack some of the councillors aligned with Paraka was of no avail. To stall his enemy at that moment, Paraka moved all his men to a new camp at Kaiwei, a few kilometres away from Mt Hagen city, then moving again around 2am the group finally settled at Lae, setting up camp at Voco Point, close to an old airport and a short walk to the city.

The rival candidates paid criminals in Lae to hijack Paraka's camp but they were unsuccessful as Paraka kept all his councillors under lock and key for their safety until they drove back to Mt Hagen for the voting process for the President Post.

Later that day, Paraka was voted as the President for Baiyer Local Level Government Council defeating the rival candidate by seven extra votes, polling 27 to his rival candidate's total of 20. After the voting, Paraka warmly thanked all his supporters who joined me in the waiting vehicles specifically hired to transport them to the councillor's home, singing victory songs along the road. The horns from the long line of vehicles kept the villagers who lived by the roadside confused and curious, wondering what had happened till they heard of Paraka's win.

I have been blessed to have such a wise and caring Uncle who has served his community with distinction and continues to do so today.

I recall meeting up with him at Kuipboat, while home on my school holidays. I congratulated him on winning the President for the Baiyer Local Level Government Council. He jokingly replied "son at last, we have made it". As we sat down near one of the trees that my father Puri had planted during the pre-independence era, he told me several things that one must learn and put into practice if he or she wants to become someone important in life.

He said, "our life is like sailing a rough sea in that our destination is unseen but patience, commitment and sacrifice will allow us to achieve our end. One must never give up hope in life. If you fail at the first attempt, you are one step closer to success, just a fingertip away".

My loving uncle spoke of Sir Edmund Hilary from New Zealand who was the first person to reach the peak of Mt Everest, the world's highest Mountain. In order to reach the top, he had overcome frostbite, hunger, and several failed attempts to make it at last. His hope, determination and desire had earned him the prize. Before we dispersed, he told me "your life is like the rising sun while mine is now like the sun about to set. I have lived and enjoyed my life because I have followed my destiny".

"Enjoy your life. Accept the good and bad because you will be sailing a rough sea and life is meant to be that way".

END

VOCABULARY

Words	Meaning
Kiaps	Australian Colonial District Administrative Officers.
Luluai	Village Chief appointed by the Australian Colonial District Administrative. Officers as mediators between the indigenous people and the Kiaps.
Kanaka	A term used by the Kiaps to refer to the indigenous people who have no knowledge about the alien concepts/European ideas.
Mena	Pig
Kyaeya	Banana.
Moka	A ceremonial pig killing and gift exchanging event in the Highlands of Papua New Guinea.
Stone axe	An axe made of stone that was used by people of some generations ago to build housed and make gardens.
Bosboi	Locals who work alongside with the Kiaps to convert the indigenous people into accepting the ideas that the foreigners introduced. "Boss Boy"
Kunai grass	A tall grass mainly found on savannah grassland areas and it is used by the indigenous people as roofs for their house.

Mini Mork	A van/truck used by the colonial administrators during the post colonial eras that can only carry a maximum passenger of two.
Kyaka	A common language spoken by the People of Baiyer. It is more or less like the language of the Enga speaking people.
Melpa	A language spoken by the rest of the Western Highlands People except the Baiyer people.
Tanem Het	A ceremonial courtship activity that involves young men and women enjoying a night out together.
Mumu	A traditional feast involves cooking of food with banana leaves and heated stones in the ground. Rock Oven.
Kyakini	A tribe in the Baiyer area of Western Highland Province where Paraka Nii and his brothers come from.
Senapun	The neighbouring tribe of Kyakini where Paraka's mother Lengame hails from.
Troepo	A tribe of the Baiyer area. It is believed that the tribes of Troepo and Kyakini have originated from one common ancestor.
Bilum	A bag made of tree barks that were used by the women to carry food and babies.
Kaukau	Is another name for Highlands sweet Potato and it is eaten by the people of Baiyer as their staple food.

Singsing	A traditional ceremonial activity that involves face painting, dancing, singing and feasting.
Kenga	A special kind of banana that is cooked only on special occasions.
Hausman	A ritual house for adult males and used for ceremonial purposes. Women are not permitted to enter this house.
Pitpit	A plant where its flower is usually eaten. It is used during feasting.
Aliyo	A Parrot that is regarded by the people of Kyakini as sacred bird and hence, it can only be seen once in every year.
Liwa liwa	A tree in the forest where its fluid is obtained to deceive and kill people. It is very dangerous and at times can cause people to be half sensed
Haus meri	It is a women's house where only the females and the babies are allowed to live.
Marlo	A traditional cloth like material used by men during singsings and other special occasions.
Tanget	It is a leaf which complements Marlo with both worn during special occasions
kun' kun,	A green which is quite often eaten raw with pork and other meats.

WITH THANKS

I especially would like to thank some people in my village and family. All of whom helped in bringing this together. I would like to thank Kila Nii for supplying some of the information which forms the basis of this novel. Mr Kerapen Nii supplied some of the photos in the book that bring fond memories to the family. And Mr Vincent Romba, thank you very much for reading the manuscript. There are so many more, with kindness and generosity helped along the way.

I would also like to express my regard and gratitude for the FNWF and their team of volunteers, for providing the platform to writers around the Greater Pacific and especially Papua New Guinea for our stories. It is an extraordinary amount of work bringing together a book of this complexity, and yet it was done; and I am grateful. Now we can share our small part of the history of Papua New Guinea; by writing our country into life.

I was at Colorado in the United States of America in 2014, during a shot visit

Nii Laik, Paraka's father at Kuipboat in 1988

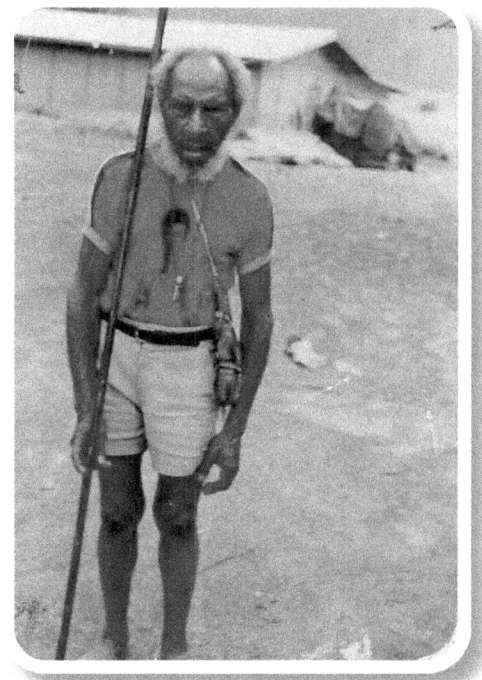

Brothers Puri and Paraka at Port Moresby during their recent visit in 2019.

My father Puri and my mother Mart'e Puri at Kuipboat in 2017

Uncle Paraka with his mother Iengame at Kuipboat in 1984

Margaret with her traditional costume.
She is Paraka's second born from his last wife.

Lengame , Paraka's mother at Kuipboat in 1986

Brothers stick together no matter what, and on the right is Puri and left Moka at Tinsley in 1976 after a soccer match. Moka is Paraka's fourth brother.

Standing at the front of the vehicle is late Michael, Paraka's half brother with some friends at Mt Hagen in 1988. Standing on the vehicle are, Joy, (middle) Ekep on the left and Nori on the right. Joy is late Michael's second wife and Ekip and Nori are from the Neighboring Senapun tribe.

My parents after a singsing event at Kumbareta in 1978, few months after they got married.

Paraka at Mt Hagen in 1984 when he was a member of the former Provincial assembly. 1984

Paraka standing ninth from left with part of the contingent that went to Philippines in 1989. As part of their visit, they went and visited Philippines Agricultural School.

Paraka with his last wife Mart and son Jeremiah on the breast at Sikisa in 1995.

Sir Julius Chan, the second Prime Minister of Papua New Guinea went to Baiyer to officially open the newly built Tinsley School of Nursing at Kumbareta in 1980. Paraka standing left with Right Honorable Sir Julius Chan. On the right facing Sir Julius Chan is the late Sai of the Maranyi tribe.

Little Trani hanging on his brother Pius' shoulder in Iaka river at Kuipboat in 1985. Trani is the second born to Paraka's second wife and Pius is the first born to Paraka's first born.

Yap on the right with his cousin the late Trapura Yaluma(middle) and his half-brother Kevin at Kuipboat in 1973. Yap is Paraka's last brother. Later Trapura is Paraka's maternal uncle from the Senapun tribe.

From left to front, the late Peng with his son late Dick and my mother and her father Enge at Dekenipana of the Ukuni lineage. My mother was around 16 years at that time and the year was 1971

Paraka at Port Moresby, the capital of Papua New Guinea during one of his random visits in 2018

Paraka with a counterpart in the Philippines, he went to Philippines including some Asian countries as a MP representing his people in the former Provincial assembly.

https://www.thenational.com.pg/wingtis-aide-honoured-with-logohu-award/

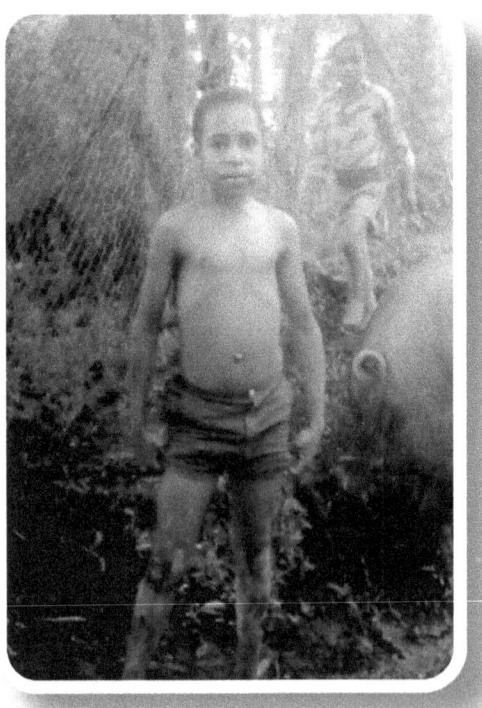

Paul Puri Nii in front and Wanbis Paraka at the back in 1989.

Seated front, from left to right Ketepa with Paraka and back row standing from left, Regina, Freda and Margaret. Regina is late Michael's (Paraka's half bother) daughter and Freda is late Peng's (Paraka's third brother) daughter and Margaret is Paraka's second daughter form his last wife.

From left to right is Gabriel Okk from the Mul lineage standing with Dawe, Nii's second wife and Paraka's stepmother and Lucky son of late Michael with Kombra a relative of Paraka and other boys in the back groud including late William Kindenge and Tony Mai.

Left to right: Trane standing with his mum Tralia sitting with little Misi and Jenny with late Marlupin on the left. They were standing Infront of John's store at Kuipboat in 1978. Trane is Paraka's second born from his second wife and Tralia is his second wife. Misi is late Marlupin's (also from Kyakin tribe) grandchild and Jenny is Paraka's fifth brother Nendepa's second daughter.

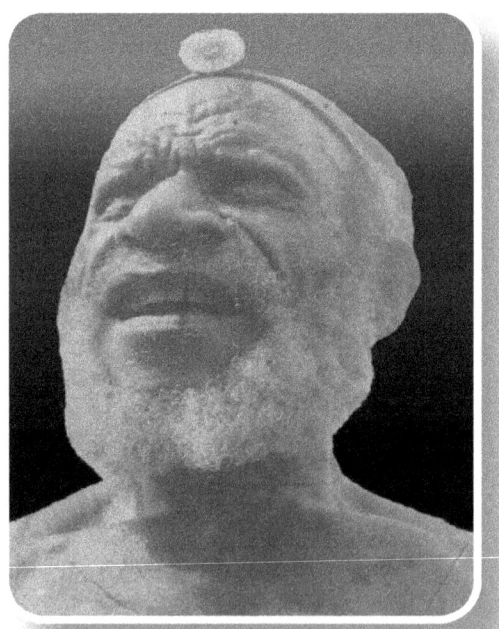

Koembo Laik, Nii's younger biological brother at Raka, a village few kilometers South west of Kuipboat.

www.ingramcontent.com/pod-product-compliance
Lightning Source LLC
Chambersburg PA
CBHW062038290426
44109CB00026B/2656